SUCCESSFUL PUBS AND INNS

Second edition

Michael Sargent and Tony Lyle

Series Editor: John O'Connor

Illustrations by Nigel Parrott

BUTTERWORTH HEINEMANN

OXFORD AMSTERDAM BOSTON LONDON NEW YORK PARIS
SAN DIEGO SAN FRANCISCO SINGAPORE SYDNEY TOKYO

Butterworth-Heinemann
An imprint of Elsevier Science
Linacre House, Jordan Hill, Oxford OX2 8DP
200 Wheeler Road, Burlington, MA 01803

First published 1994
Reprinted 1996
Second edition 1998
Transferred to digital printing 2003

British Library Cataloguing in Publication Data
A catalogue record for this book is available from the British Library

ISBN 0 7506 4113 4

Printed and bound in Great Britain by Antony Rowe Ltd, Eastbourne

Contents

Preface

We have written this book for use by practising innkeepers and for those seeking to make a career in the licensed trade. We have highlighted the things that separate the successful from the unsuccessful.

It is a practical book, free of jargon, written in an easy-to-read style. We have drawn on our knowledge of actual publicans and real situations to illustrate the points we are making. You do not need to be a scholar to get value from this book but you will need to be fully committed to innkeeping, believing passionately in customer care and quality of product to get the full benefit from it.

In a book of this size, it is not possible to cover all subjects thoroughly. If you want to learn how to cook, how to do bookkeeping or the finer techniques of marketing, you will find specific books in this series covering these subjects. We have tried to put these and other subjects into context so that their importance to the business is fully understood. We have suggested, where necessary, that expert advice is sought and from where it can be obtained.

We use the word 'innkeeper' a great deal but, if you feel more comfortable with the terms 'landlord', 'landlady', 'licensee' or 'publican', please substitute them in your own mind. Although we have dealt with each subject principally in one chapter, we do return to the same subject in subsequent chapters. The index at the back of the book is a full one and will give a page number for each reference to any particular subject.

There are quite significant regional differences in pubs and inns and drinking habits. In the north of England, beer drinking, especially of cask-conditioned northern bitters, is higher than in the south. In Scotland little cask-conditioned beer is drunk but volumes of lager and keg ales are high; not surprisingly, whisky sales are also considerable. Northern, Welsh and Scottish readers may occasionally find a touch of southern bias but, we hope, not too much.

This book was originally written in the wake of the implementation of the Tied Estate Orders with the industry consequently in a state of flux. The rate of change shows no signs of abating with groups of pubs switching ownership with bewildering regularity; well known brewers selling their breweries and others merging their brewing interests. The huge growth in branded 'super-pubs' increases the pressure on individual innkeepers. Although the growth of food sales in pubs has created new opportunities, overall, the trading conditions are difficult.

We still recommend innkeeping as a career but only if you are totally committed; are sure you have the talent; have obtained sufficient training and gained enough experience to make it work. The best innkeepers are doing very well – many others fail.

We have made ourselves pests with our many friends in the trade by seeking their opinions on some of the more difficult sections of this book. They are too numerous to mention but we know who they are and they know who they are and we are very grateful to them. We would, though, like to thank our illustrator, Nigel Parrott, for his excellent work. He produced each drawing exactly to specification, without delay, with no fuss and for less than the price of a pint. That is the kind of pub design surveyor that all of us would like to work with!

Michael Sargent
Tony Lyle

1 So you want to run a pub?

The dream of many people over the years has been to give up their nine-to-five job and take a pub or country inn. Their vision was of foaming tankards of ale, of delicious freshly prepared food and customers queuing to get into their car park at opening time. The reality was often very different.

Today, more than ever before, licensed retailing demands specific talents from special people. This applies whether you are a salaried manager, a tenant licensee or the owner/operator of the premises.

Motives

Those who interview for prospective managers or tenants have, with good reason, come to be suspicious of certain sentences from the applicants before them:

- 'I want to escape from the rat race.'
- 'All our friends say we'd be marvellous at it.'
- 'We're retiring soon and think it would be nice to run a pub.'
- 'I've just been made redundant and decided to run a pub.'
- 'It's a business and a roof over our heads as well.'
- 'My husband has always wanted to run a pub.'
- 'I'm a senior manager in industry so I certainly should be capable of just running a pub.'

These are the people who do not understand what entering the licensed trade means; such attitudes are unacceptable as a basis for starting out upon a whole new way of life. Sadly, though, we can all quickly think of landlords who have slipped through the net and both they and their customers are suffering for it.

To be successful in the trade, you need:

- dedication to the ideal of customer service;
- to have a burning desire to build your business;
- to welcome hard work and long hours;
- to be able to relate well to customers and staff;
- to enjoy the financial challenge of running a largely cash business where control of that cash and of your food and liquor stocks is critical.

The list could go on but the point we are making is that innkeeping is a complex mix of talents and skills. No one should believe that it is simple and should not expect easy pickings from it. It is a tough, competitive business.

Objectives

You need to be honest with yourself as to your objectives in the trade. Are you there to:

- offer a service to the community
- primarily make money
- enjoy a certain lifestyle
- exploit your particular talents for hospitality;

or

- be your own boss?

The best answer may be a mix of all of these and a few more besides; successful innkeepers and publicans are blessed with a similarly wide range of abilities.

Skills

In the not so recent past, the licensed trade was often seen as the home of the amateur. People spoke of 'retiring and taking a pub' as though it was something that anyone could do. Happily, this unthinking approach is now much more rare. A good licensee today needs many skills encompassing:

- personnel management to recruit, retain and inspire staff;
- the creation of a hospitable environment for customers;
- financial management to fully understand the way the business operates and to influence the profitability of the business;
- relating to customers and understanding their needs;
- giving first-class customer service;
- marketing skills to attract new custom;
- technical skills to run a good cellar and to operate a kitchen producing quality food punctually and consistently.

If you add to all this the job knowledge required, such as a basic understanding of wine, the law in respect of hygiene, health and safety, licensing, employment, VAT, PAYE and tax, you can see that being a licensee of even the most ordinary backstreet pub is a highly skilled profession.

Increasingly, the licensed and catering trades will be seeking people with qualifications. The introduction of S/NVQs (Scottish/national vocational qualifications) is only one step in that direction.

There are a number of training courses on offer; the larger brewers and pub companies (pubcos as the trade press like to describe them) put their own licensed house managers through extensive training programmes and various organizations regularly advertise their courses for budding or existing licensees in the trade press. Selected colleges and universities are in the forefront of training for all aspects of the 'hospitality business'.

Ever more important is the National Licensee's Certificate, awarded by the British Institute of Innkeeping (BII), described later in this chapter under 'A fit and proper person'.

Experience

However good the training, there is no substitute for experience. It is difficult for an outsider to understand the various aspects of operating an inn or pub without having spent some time working in one. No training course or manual can adequately convince you of how tired you will be during your first few weeks, how long the day will seem or how it will feel behind your bar or in your kitchen for the first time.

A salaried manager with a brewery company or pub operator will have been through not only a training course of perhaps twelve weeks or more but also a period of many months carrying out relief management in a variety of houses. This is invaluable as it allows him or her to obtain practical experience in all aspects of innkeeping but without a long-term obligation to the particular inn or pub he or she is running while the full-time licensee is on holiday. During these periods, he or she will have been under general supervision but will have had day-to-day responsibility for the operation of the business.

Anyone entering the trade is well advised to devote as much time as possible to obtaining this type of experience. Work in a similar establishment to the one you intend running, not for just a few hours but sufficient to give a real understanding of the future business. It may be necessary to work free for a quality operator to get this experience but this is surely better than investing your capital into a business and then finding that you cannot handle it. Working in that friendly pub may look very different from the inside and may well dispel the cosy dream you had as a customer. Most companies when interviewing prospective tenant licensees will expect the candidate to have some worthwhile practical experience in the trade so it really has to be considered an essential part of your preparation for this new way of life.

Health and stamina

In any business, good health is important. If you are self-employed, it is even more so. If you run a pub, your health is critical. In most establishments, the character and personality of the landlord are significant not only in setting the style and tone of the business but also in relating directly to the customers.

Market research projects tend to highlight the character of the landlord as a major factor in the customer's decision to visit. It follows that the landlord's presence is essential to the continuing success of the business: they cannot afford too many days off for sickness. The long hours, seven-day opening and physical nature of much of the work is tough. Standing behind the bar or working in the restaurant or kitchen, often at high temperatures, is demanding. Of course, work for the owner or manager is not limited to opening hours; there is much to be done before and after customers leave. A twelve-hour working day is quite usual.

So you just have to be physically healthy!

There is another sort of pressure that is put upon innkeepers, particularly those who run their business in a personal way, who are in their premises most of the time and indeed 'live over the shop'. These are often the people who are the most outgoing and are greatly liked by their customers – the 'mine host' par excellence. The total commitment to the business can become overpowering so that, when off duty, there is no escape. Many licensees will tell you that their greatest wish is to 'have their own front door', to be free and away from the public, even for a few hours.

One cannot leave the subject of health without mentioning the hazards of over-indulgence. Most inns and many pubs have food available much of the time. The temptation for the innkeeper to eat too much or at the wrong time is a potential problem. The temptation to drink to excess is even more obvious. Alcohol is readily available, the inn a sociable place and the licensee is expected to be part of it. Few innkeepers are teetotal but the majority drink sensibly. They have to or it could destroy them and their business.

So you need to be not just physically healthy but mentally tough as well!

Temperament

It is hard to generalize about the temperament needed for success in the licensed trade but it helps to be calm in a crisis, even-tempered with awkward customers or recalcitrant staff, clear-headed when making financial judgements and patient when listening to the same often-told story from a regular. All quite saint-like really! But perhaps you will also need a bit of ego when wishing to be the best, a touch of anger when standards fall below your own high standards and total intolerance of staff who do not, after all your patient coaching, understand the importance of customer care.

The great majority of inns and pubs are run by a man and woman team. The stress on a marriage or other personal relationship is often extreme. The demands of the business, seven days a week, can draw them in different and sometimes conflicting directions. In spite of their parents being in the building most of the time, children can sometimes feel neglected. Their parents are torn between the needs of their family and those of their customers and this causes more friction. The lack of privacy, because of the 'goldfish bowl' existence, can add to pressures. Most couples row from time to time but innkeepers have to somehow keep it private because nothing is picked up more quickly than an 'atmosphere' and this is certainly bad for trade.

The need for each partner to have at least some of the saintly qualities is essential but, as readers of John Fothergill's *An Innkeeper's Diary* will know, there is an exception to every rule!

A fit and proper person

To be a licensee as manager, tenant or owner, you need to hold a justice's licence. Initially, you are likely to be applying to the Licensing Bench of the local magistrates court for a Protection Order (a form of provisional licence) and then for a full transfer of the 'licence to sell liquor for consumption on or off the premises'. At either of these stages, you may be quizzed by the magistrates on your ability to run the public house named in your application. The police may visit you at home and will make computer enquiries regarding your possible criminal record. If they find a blemish on your record, then they may well object to your licence application in court. Alcohol-related offences, handling and receiving stolen goods and crimes of violence during the previous ten years would make a successful application unlikely. If you have a conviction, it is much better to declare it and personally speak to the police and, if possible, the Clerk to the Justices, to see beforehand if your application has any chance of success. Even if you have no conviction but are known to have been associating with undesirables, the police may still object and magistrates normally will take full note of their objection. Magistrates are now going further and will often wish to assure themselves that you have sufficient training and experience to be able to run an 'orderly house'.

The National Licensee's Certificate was introduced by the British Institute of Innkeeping (BII) with the aim of raising standards of those already running or intent on running a public house. The Certificate is awarded to those who pass the examination covering basic licensing law and the social responsibilities of licensees. Courses are organized in various parts of the country; to succeed in the examination demands commitment and application but it is not in itself overly difficult.

The important fact is that magistrates in many licensing districts are now looking on the National Licensee's Certificate as a prime factor in assessing an applicant's merit and in some cases are reluctant to grant a justice's licence unless the Certificate, or an approved training qualification, is held.

The assessments by the licensing benches may vary in different parts of the country but they all have the aim of deciding whether the applicant is, in the traditional phrase 'a fit and proper person' to hold a justice's licence.

Appearing in court

For some inexperienced applicants, appearing before the licensing magistrates may be a daunting experience. Make sure you are well briefed in advance and understand the procedures. Most licensing committees have a policy document which it would be wise to obtain for your own guidance. You may choose to use a solicitor or a licensed house broker in court. Be appropriately dressed, observe the etiquette of the court, address individual justices as 'Sir' or 'Madam', speak clearly and confidently.

It is not only for Protection Orders and Full Transfers that you may need to appear in court. Your Justice's Licence is subject to renewal at the tri-annual licensing meetings (the Brewster Sessions) in February 2001 and three yearly thereafter.

Existing licensees or licence holders in the previous three years of good repute, may benefit from the streamlining of the system when applying to move to a different pub. Such an application for the transfer of a licence may be granted administratively by the Clerk to the Licensing Justices (the person whom the justices rely on for interpreting the law) and granted outside of licensing sessions, thus bypassing the cumbersome Protection Order procedures.

Rewards

There has been much in this chapter about the demands of the licensed trade. What of the rewards?

Non-material rewards

To be successful as an innkeeper, you have to enjoy what you are doing. Bad-tempered, gloomy people running pubs and inns are almost certain to fail.

- One of the greatest rewards therefore is in doing the job well and experiencing the immediate pleasure of seeing customers happy, satisfied and becoming regular patrons of your establishment.
- There is the reward of a smoothly, professionally run business where you are the driving force.
- You will get huge satisfaction from seeing the team of hard-working staff that you have gathered around you putting into practice all the customer skills that you have taught them.

- You will be providing employment, often in a small rural community, and you may well become the biggest employer in the area.
- As a successful businessman or woman operating what has become an important social centre, you will have, quite naturally, a certain standing in the community. In a village, you are likely to be as well known as the doctor and perhaps better known than the vicar. The degree to which you wish to involve yourself in the local community is up to you but it may well be bad business to cut yourself off from your neighbours.
- If you are a tenant or an owner, you will have the added satisfaction of being your own boss, running your life and your business in tandem. To an extent, you can organize your business to suit yourself.
- Most customers who choose to visit you either to eat or drink will be in a sociable mood. If you provide the ambience that pleases them, you will be in the happy position of working amongst cheerful people – a rare bonus for any businessman or businesswoman.
- Most successful innkeepers actually like most of their customers. It is often said that a landlord gathers people similar to himself into his pub. This means that, with luck, you may well be surrounded by people whom you would otherwise consider friends and who will be paying money to visit you. A wonderful concept for the frugal yet sociable business person!

Material rewards

It is not possible to generalize about the amount of money a business will make although this book will, we hope, steer our readers in the right direction. There is no guarantee that any pub or inn will make a profit for its licensee. Indeed, a feature of the early 1990s was the desperate struggle of literally thousands of licensed businesses to survive.

However, given the right pub in a good location and skilled professional management, the business should be profitable. Before allowing for loan repayments or rent, an efficient inn or pub can make a net profit of well over 20 per cent and even as much as 30 per cent of VAT-exclusive turnover. These ratios do not work well with low-taking houses but tend to get progressively better as takings get higher.

Innkeeping is a profession that demands a great deal; the rewards are most often related not just to the effort but to the high levels of skill and flair exhibited by the real enthusiasts. It is not good enough to 'try your best' if your best is not as good as your competitors.

2 What type of pub do you want?

If you are taking your first pub or considering your next move within the licensed trade, it will be to your advantage to have an overview on the structure of the trade. If you are to negotiate a worthwhile deal for yourself, it will be in your interests to understand how the system works and what are the prime objectives of the companies letting and selling pubs and inns. Only with this information will you be able to make a judgement as to whether the deal you have struck is the best one available.

There are currently over 58,000 pubs in Britain. Of these more than 42,000 are owned by brewers and pub companies and over 16,000 are freehouses. Ten years ago, the major players such as Allied Domecq, Bass, Courage, Grand Metropolitan, Scottish & Newcastle and Whitbread owned around 25,000 pubs. Due to mergers and forced sales this number has been halved and the new major pub companies such as Pubmaster, Enterprise Inns, Greenalls, Grovebase and the Grand Pub Company now operate a similar number of pubs to the remaining major brewers. Some of the regional brewers have built up their pub estates significantly. Greene King, Wolverhampton & Dudley, Marston and Vaux own over 4,000 between them. Mansfield, Ushers, Thwaites, Morland and Burtonwood each own around 500 pubs, as do pub companies such as Inn Business and Century Inns. What all have in common is a stiff neck from looking over their shoulders, in case they are the next subject of a takeover.

So pub ownership and brewery suppliers are sure to remain in a state of flux for the foreseeable future, therefore if you are looking for an industry in which little changes from year to year then look for something more stable like film directing!

The majority of pubs and inns come under the following headings:

- managed houses;
- brewery-tied tenancies;
- brewery-tied leases;
- independent pub-operating companies tied tenancies;
- free leases;
- freehold free houses.

Before we cover these in detail, it will help to explore at greater length what is 'tied trade':

- its background;
- why did it develop?
- what effect have recent events and legislation had upon it?
- a little of the politics of it.

Background to the tied trade

The tied trade system has dominated the industry throughout the twentieth century and it has only been during the last decade that major changes have been seen.

Brewery-owned pubs and exclusive supply agreements have been with us for around 200 years. In spite of all its defects, the system has served the public and the landlords well. It has helped give a modest living to landlords in small pubs and has ensured that many pubs which are now considered unviable were kept open for the benefit of the local population.

A series of major mergers between brewers since the war alarmed the Monopolies and Mergers Commission (MMC). It tried, on several occasions, to bring in more competition both on brands and pricing but, in the main, the moves it made have had an adverse effect and reduced, rather than increased, choice for the general public.

Until the mid-1960s, rents of public houses tended to be low with the brewers getting most of their income from beer, wines and spirits that were sold to tenants at above normal wholesale price. Since that time, with the value of properties escalating and the cost of repairs becoming a greater drain on resources, the rents have been increasing quite dramatically. A typical rent for a country inn during the 1960s might have been £200 a year whereas that same property might well cost at least twice as much as that each week now! Brewers, particularly the major ones, have been under pressure to make their assets work harder and rents now tend to reflect the value of the property.

In spite of rising rents, the wholesale price of products increased ahead of inflation and pump prices increased even more to help innkeepers pay the extra rent demanded of them. This, and a perceived lack of competition, culminated in the Tied Estate Orders which were fully implemented in November 1992.

The Tied Estate Orders and other government rulings

There have been several government-sponsored MMC reports and inquiries into the brewing industry mainly attempting to tackle the problem of vertically integrated companies which manufacture, distribute, wholesale and retail their products through their wholly owned properties. This clearly gives the opportunity to control prices and to restrict choice. The problem is that, with all its faults, it has been difficult to find a system that works better. Most reports finished up gathering dust because the government Trade Secretary of the day could see the dangers in them. Lord Young was the exception when he stood up in the Commons in 1989 and said 'I am minded to accept this report'. Those seven words brought about disruption and changes of a magnitude never seen before.

The six major brewers, dominant in the late eighties, had to sell, or lease free from tie, 50 per cent of all houses they owned over 2,000. During the three years to November 1992, thousands of pubs changed hands. The smaller regional brewers bought up groups of pubs ranging from just a handful up to more than 100. Because the MMC report was thought through so badly, it has done little to break local monopolies – indeed, it has helped create some new ones. It could have been so much more effective had pub ownership within postal codes or licensing districts been restricted to a given percentage.

Many new multiple pub owners were created from the giant sell-off. The pubs purchased were mainly the bottom end of the major brewers' estates and often bought at bargain basement prices. These pub companies mainly operate their pubs as tenancies deriving their income from the rents they charge and the large discount they obtain from their supplying brewers. Not much of this discount is passed on to their tenants. There are many poor pubs amongst them and these pubs are bad news whoever owns them. So if you are considering taking a pub that has had three licensees during the last five years take very great care!

A more positive result has come from the pub companies that operate their growing estates through managers. Excellent examples are Wetherspoons, Yates's and Regent Inns. These, together with smaller groups such as Slug and Lettuce (Grosvenor Inns) and Pitcher and Piano (now Marstons) have set new standards that have to be matched by the rest. It seems likely, though, that these companies would have developed anyway, without government intervention.

It is also a fact that the sell-off gave a unique opportunity for individuals, including sitting tenants, to buy a pub as a free house, often at an advantageous price. Many of these have been developed by their new owners and the circle completed when they have been sold on again to family brewers or pub companies.

Types of operation

Having looked briefly at the background and some of the influences on today's licensed trade, we now move on to the types of licensed houses that a licensee or aspiring innkeeper may wish to operate.

Managed houses

Most brewers of any size operate managed houses as do an increasing number of pub operating companies with no brewing interests.

The freeholder or leaseholder appoints a manager to run the pub. The manager is paid a salary and usually receives a performance-related bonus. Accommodation in the pub is normally offered or alternative housing if it is a lock-up. The manager has no financial stake in the business but is responsible to the employer for the day-to-day running and financial control of the pub.

The advantages of being a manager are earning a regular salary, no requirement for capital except perhaps a small security deposit and the entitlement to regular and quite generous holidays. As manager, an innkeeper often has the opportunity of running a bigger and better pub than as an owner, and enjoys the prestige of operating a major business.

The downside of managing is that the pressures on profit generation and exceedingly stretching budgets year after year can take away much of the pleasure from the work. Although there are many aids to stock control, it is still the manager's responsibility to produce good stock results. Many managers lose their jobs through lack of control, and job security is therefore not good.

Nevertheless, it is by far the best way of learning the pub business and very few managers, who have the entrepreneurial spirit to branch out on their own, fail to make a success of their own business.

Brewery-owned tenancies

This is the best option for an aspiring licensee with a small amount of capital. It involves you in a series of interviews with the brewery concerned, usually in competition with others. If you are the one selected, you will be expected to buy the trade inventory, saleable stock and glassware at valuation. The brewery will probably take a security deposit from you as insurance against your being unable to pay your brewery account or rent at some future time.

The minimum capital required could be as little as £10,000 but for reasons that we will expand on later, there is little chance of this size of business giving a reasonable living. Most tenanted 'ingoings' are in the £15,000 to £35,000 range. It does not necessarily follow that, the more you pay, the better the business. Actual and potential turnover are the principal assessments that need to be made when looking at a tenanted proposition.

With a tenancy, you will have a limited repair obligation. In the main, this will cover internal decorations and minor repairs. In some cases, the brewery might require you to take on external decorations and more extensive repairs and you need to be very clear what your obligations will be. Some brewers prefer to decorate and repair all the public areas of the property and do not allow you to repaint the bar for instance. Read the agreement carefully and do not be afraid of asking questions.

The brewery tenancy agreement will have some form of supply arrangement known as 'the tie'. With small and regional brewers, this covers all beers and lagers. Many of them will supply you with other brewers' 'guest' ales and probably a national lager but all bought exclusively from them. The tie on low-alcohol beers, ciders, wine, spirits and minerals is now less widespread but the smaller breweries, which produce annual volumes of beer below a prescribed limit, have far greater freedom to tie their tenants.

You pay a rent to the brewer and this is normally reviewed three-yearly. The rent levels can vary quite widely and are usually assessed on the turnover or expected turnover of the pub. Some agreements will allow you to keep all of the AWP (amusement with profit, i.e. fruit machine) income after paying the rent to the machine owner and this needs to be taken into account when comparing pub rents.

You may receive some discount on beer supplies but you are excluded from taking advantage of the major discounts that are available to the free trade.

The advantages of tenancies are that, for a modest and reasonably risk-free investment, you can run your own business. Although you have some obligations to the brewery that owns the property, you are free to develop the style of business that suits you. Any profit, after paying your rent and other outgoings, is yours. Many tenants have made a good living over the years and there are still good tenancies to be had.

The downside is that the pub is never going to be your own. You cannot sell the business, just the inventory and stock, so, if you have doubled the turnover, this will not benefit you when you decide to leave. The agreements are rather restrictive and do not allow you to buy beer supplies at the best prices. The property is not yours to improve and that may well stop you expanding the business.

The non-brewery-tied tenancy

There are several thousand pubs operating under these agreements. Because they do not own breweries, the companies do not have any restriction on the number of pubs as dictated by the Tied Estate Orders. They enter into supply agreements with brewers and often make an attractive range of beers available to their tenants. Their agreements vary widely and particular care should be taken in understanding the tenant's obligations, especially on repairs.

As already mentioned these companies derive their income from two main sources:

- rent;
- discounts from their supplying breweries.

Currently, the discounts are very high but, as the major brewers cut back on brewing capacity, discounts could fall and cause severe difficulties to some of the pub-operating companies.

Some companies were initially short of cash and could not afford to repair and redecorate the dilapidated pubs they had acquired. Consequently, many pubs were trading well below their real potential. During the late 1990s however they have been spending more freely and their estates have gradually been put into better shape.

The brewery-tied lease

This was a small segment of the trade up to the mid-1980s. Inntrepreneur led the way in this market, picking up much criticism in the process. Following the Tied Estate Orders, Allied Domecq (Vanguard lease), Whitbread (Pub Partnership) and Bass (Bass lease) fully committed themselves to pub leasing. By the end of the 1990s, however, first Inntrepreneur and then Bass sold their interests in leased properties. Some regional and family brewers developed their own style of lease but many of these were non-assignable and more like tenancies than true leases.

The leases tend to be from ten to twenty years with rent reviews at regular intervals of either three or five years. They are usually assignable which means, if a buyer can be found, the lease can be sold on. The person taking on the lease, known as the lessee, assumes full responsibility for the repairs and decorations to the property. Most have 'put and keep' clauses for repairs which means the lessee has a legal obligation to put the property in good repair and keep it that way.

They are all tied for ales and lagers but, by law, the major brewers have a provision that allows the lessee to purchase a guest ale from a supplier of his choice. On some leases, discounts are offered over agreed target figures.

It is essential to plan your application fully for one of these leases. You must take advice and produce a business plan with takings and profit figures that you are confident of achieving. You need to make an assessment as to the likely level of repairs and, if you are offered the pub, go to the expense of having a full costed structural survey done. If the rent being asked is higher than you can safely afford and you cannot get the company to reduce it, you must not proceed. If you get your sums wrong, then you can finish up bankrupt.

There has been a reasonable market in leases over the last few years with prices often commanding a premium (a premium is the difference between the value of the inventory and price paid for a lease). The free of tie leasehold market is especially buoyant on pubs trading well, as these are often attractive to family brewers and pub companies as well as to individuals. If, however, the pub is trading badly and making a loss then it is usually difficult to find a buyer at any price.

Privity of contract was an unfair clause inserted in most leases (not just pubs) but happily it has been outlawed in recent years. It meant that even after lessees had assigned their interest in a lease, the lessors could sue them for rent and repairs if the new lessee subsequently got into financial difficulties. Do check with your solicitor on this point before assigning, as the clause could still be in your current lease.

Leases can be very worthwhile. For a reasonably modest outlay, they can give you the chance of creating a first-class business. If you build turnover and profits then the lease will start to accumulate a useful capital value. You have the chance, with your landlord's permission, to make alterations to the property that then help the business grow even more.

The dangers are obvious and this is no place for the amateur. You must negotiate a sensible deal at the outset or you may never be able to make a profit. You should consult:

- an accountant,
- a solicitor,
- a chartered surveyor,

or, if you can find one, your own lease negotiator who will steer you through from start to finish.

The free lease

These were a rare opportunity until the 1990s. They were licensed properties offered on lease by city and borough councils, by colleges, by property companies and occasionally by individuals. Inntrepreneur Estates entered this market in a big way in the first half of the 1990s, freeing up hundreds of their previously tied estate.

The main difference between tied and free leases is quite obvious. With a free lease, you can buy all your supplies from a brewer of your choice. There is a great advantage in being able to buy in the free market. If you are running a rural inn or any establishment where 'real ale' is a major influence, then being free can give you the choice of product and therefore a competitive advantage. We will cover discounts and other free-trade benefits later in this chapter. These can be substantial and an important source of revenue. There are still a few excellent opportunities around, especially if you are able to find a free lease with high beer sales.

The major problems with free leases are basically the same as for tied leases except the rent is likely to be substantially higher. The higher rent will take account of the additional benefits that are available to the 'free trader'. You still need to be just as careful at the outset to get the right deal on rent and to have taken full account of the repair liability that you are taking on.

The freehold free house

Most aspiring innkeepers dream of owning their own free house. For many years, the value of free houses continued to escalate and ownership became a very profitable venture. The brewery pubs sell-off shattered many dreams as values plummeted when supply far outweighed demand. The price of the average free house is now quite sensible and it is an opportunity that is open to many more people than before.

This type of opportunity allows owners total freedom to develop and operate the pub as they wish, subject only to planning and licensing permissions.

A freehold free house is normally bought with a mortgage of up to 66 per cent of its valuation. It does mean therefore that more of your own capital is needed for this type of business. Prices range from £60,000 upwards but, like most businesses, the lower the price, the smaller the opportunity.

Discounts and other free-trade benefits

Discounting in the free-trade market rises and falls in line with brewery capacity and the quest for market share. All the major brewers at present are discounting heavily and all agree that they have too many breweries and are capable of producing at least a third more beer if there was a market for it.

Higher discounts are available to those with reasonably high beer throughputs of, say, 300 plus barrels per year. Usually, lager carries a higher discount than ale and it is currently possible to receive well over £65 a barrel on lager and more than £40 on ales. A rather obvious point, but one that is often overlooked, is the need to check the base wholesale price. There is very little point getting an extra £5 per barrel discount if the wholesale price is £10 dearer!

From time to time, advance discount schemes are on offer. In these, a brewery may give you £5,000 or so for improvements and allow you to repay it with your discounts over a given period. The discounts are usually a little lower than average but it can be a helpful source of cash in the early days of a business.

Breweries will sometimes loan the money to help purchase the business secured by a first or second mortgage. The interest rates are usually around 5 per cent but the savings in interest are normally offset by an equivalent reduction in beer discounts. The brewers were badly caught out on these loans when free house prices slumped in the late 1980s and are consequently more cautious these days. It is worth getting a quote from one or more brewers, however, and weighing it up against what another lender would charge you and what discounts would then be available.

Brewers offer what they term as plant on loan. This can vary from cellar cooling equipment to bar furnishings. This type of deal was very popular for many years and is sometimes still available. You 'pay off' the loan by purchasing a given number of barrels a year for a specified period from that brewer.

Promotional packages are generous and sometimes exciting. Some are designed to allow you to have good promotional nights for your customers and others are aimed directly at the licensee. It is not unusual to 'win' expensive presents or foreign travel and, without sounding too grasping, it is worth asking about this form of activity when deciding upon your supplier.

Wholesalers have become increasingly competitive. They supply products from a range of different companies. Many can give a full service by supplying all beers, ciders, soft drinks, wines and spirits on one vehicle and with one invoice. They are quite prepared to offer a discount for total supply that may well match or better those of individual brewing, soft drink or wine and spirit companies.

Credit terms are usually better in the free trade than in the tied. Average credit terms are payments two weeks after the end of the month in which the supplies were made. If you order more heavily earlier in the month and very lightly at the end, you will find this a valuable source of cash flow. Credit terms in the tied estates average around two weeks.

Beer dispense equipment is usually loaned by the supplying company. They will also put in some sophisticated beer line cleaning and in-line cooling equipment if your trade warrants it. This type of equipment costs several thousand pounds so it is an important concession. If you subsequently change your main brewer, he will sell on his cellar equipment to the incoming brewer.

Special offers are another feature of the free trade. You could well find offers of a free keg of beer with four bought when business is slack. Sadly, the free-trade market has little place in it for loyalty and, as long as you do not upset your customers by changing brewers, you need to constantly try and get the best deal.

Who's who in the tied trade?

The majority of innkeepers operate a brewery-owned or pub-owning-company pub. Even to the most confident, the process of obtaining a pub from this source is daunting. Although the view within these companies is that everyone has too much to do, to the would-be innkeeper, there appear to be dozens of area managers, district managers, business-development managers, district sales managers, leasing managers, estate managers, regional or trade directors, not to mention their agents. This can all put off the average couple who just want to get on with running their own business and looking after their customers.

One of the jobs of all those listed above is to attempt to get the right person into the right pub. For all that you may perceive as their faults, this is what they are really trying to do.

The key person in the affair is usually the one who will be judged on the success of the pub. Although you may well have a second interview with a director, it is the area manager, or whatever the equivalent title is at the time, who you really have to convince. Very few directors will override the view of the area manager who is to be monitored on the success of the pub.

Area managers are busy and like their applicants have to be organized. They do not like ten-page CVs when the information could go on to one page. They like well-thought-through business plans that illustrate that you are reading the pub's market and potential correctly. Couples who allow each other to speak and have complementary skills are a delight to them. They are impressed when you tell them you have visited all the competitor houses more than once and have found a market gap for the pub in question. If you make your presentation in a professional and organized way, your chances of being successful are greatly enhanced. Make their job easy for them and they are more likely to come up with the right decision and offer the pub to you!

Summary

If you possibly can, learn your business as a manager for one of the big companies and then, once you feel ready, risk your own cash on a business of your own.

Read and understand the agreement that is on offer. Pay particular attention to the level of your repair obligations.

If you are buying your own freehold, weigh up all the options open to you. Although a brewery low-interest loan may sound attractive, check it out against the discounts on beers that you could be losing.

There are still some good opportunities within the licensed trade as long as you do your homework well enough. It is no place for the amateur and it is now much harder to make money. There is no substitute for experience and you should always work within the trade before signing yourself up into a long-term agreement.

3 The choice is yours

The right pub

So you have decided to take a pub. You now understand the structure of the industry but you still need to be sure that you find the right pub, one that you will be happy in and that will earn you money. All sorts of pubs can earn profits but a pub with an unhappy licensee is rarely successful.

The right geography

You have to decide on the geography. Where do you want to be: north or south, town or country, main road or back street, industrial area or rural backwater?

A pub that suits you

You have to choose the type of pub in which you feel temperamentally comfortable. Remember, you are not just visiting this pub as a customer but are committing yourself and probably your family to living on the premises for seven days a week and serving the customers virtually every day of the year.

You may not achieve your ideal but you must know what your ideal is and how far you are prepared to depart from it before you start the serious matter of seeking out the business that will be your home as well as your livelihood, perhaps for many years to come.

The right site in the right location

There is an old saying that three things are needed when buying a house: location, location and location. The same can be said about pubs but this time it is site and location. Get these two factors right and find a pub that suits its site and location and you are likely to succeed. Although we all know of remote inns that always seem to be packed to the doors, these are the exception. Badly located pubs usually trade badly.

A good location

What is a good location? It is one in which the pub is comfortably reached by sufficient customers to make the business successful. This is obvious but true, for it is no use having a pub with 2,000 potential customers within walking distance if they all have to cross a four-lane highway to reach it – or a roadside country pub on the wrong side of a fast and dangerous bend – or a tucked-away pub where the authorities will not allow a sign to be put up saying where it is.

Through the eyes of the customer

When evaluating a pub, look at it as a customer would. How would you reach it? How easy and attractive is getting to it? How many other customers would find it? What appeals to you is quite likely to appeal to people like you.

Pub types and how to recognize them

So far, we have only talked of a 'pub' but there are over 50,000 of them in Britain. The beauty of British pubs is their variety, so how on earth do you set about choosing one from so many?

You will have noticed the growth of pub brands. Companies are now able to market a particular style of pub in similar way to a brand of cornflakes or a make of motor car. A Wetherspoons pub is instantly recognizable, as is a Yates's Wine Bar, an O'Neill's or a Firkin pub. These together with branded local pubs such as Mr Qs (Allied), John Barras (Scottish & Newcastle Retail) and food-led outlets such as Brewer's Fayre (Whitbread), Miller's Kitchen (Greenalls) and Vintage Inns (Bass), now dominate the pub market.

All these pub brands were born from a form of pub segmentation. Segmentation is a way of grouping similar types of pubs together and by so doing, understanding them and the customers they cater for that much better.

It is easy enough to spot the difference between a youngsters' pub with music five nights a week and a lovely country pub with a thriving food business. But others are not quite that obvious. We believe that the majority of all pubs could be 'typecast' in the following way. It is likely that you personally will only be suitable for, and enjoy running, one or two of the following styles of pubs.

The estate local

This type of pub (see Figure 3.1) will be located in the middle of a housing estate, either council or private/council mixed. It will probably have been built between 1950 and 1975, will be spacious, with a good car park but little or no pub garden. There will be no worthwhile food sales, but sales of crisps, nuts and cigarettes will be high. AWPs (fruit machines), video games, juke box and pool tables will be important sources of income. One or two keg beers, a smooth flow (nitro-keg as the Campaign for Real Ale calls them), a standard lager and a

Figure 3.1

premium lager will be the major sellers. Sales of cask conditioned beers will be quite low in the south but a little higher in the north of England.

Customers will be mainly male and usually aged 25 plus. Darts and pool teams are important and often soccer teams are supported by the pub. The landlord must understand the local community and work with it.

Some of these pubs can be rough and even violent.

The general local

This type of pub (see Figure 3.2) can be found on through roads on the outskirts of large towns, on the side of major estates or sometimes in the centre of small towns and large villages. They often have one bar and good car parking. Food sales are important particularly at lunchtime. Allied's Big Steak pubs have extended the sale of food into the evening sessions but often at the expense of pool and darts which would otherwise be important to this segment. Lagers, both standard and premium, enjoy major sales as do draught stout and smooth flow ales. Cask conditioned ales have an important place in the sales mix.

Customers will mainly live within three miles of the pub and arrive by car. A wide age group upwards from 20 will be catered for with a 70/30 ratio in favour of males in the early part of the week but reducing to 60/40 over the weekend and at lunchtimes.

The General Local

Figure 3.2

The traditional inn

This section is represented by the classic English pub (see Figure 3.3), with a rural location, the most successful being found within ten minutes' drive of a large town. Good car parking is usually available at the pub or nearby and a well-kept and well-used pub garden. It has often been converted to one bar with beams, brasses, intimate lighting and often log fires. There is lots of 'atmosphere', and no AWPs or juke box. Food is most important at lunchtime but less so in the evening. Customers are mainly white collar workers and retired people at lunchtime and in the evening a wider range of couples tending to be smart and younger.

A variation on the traditional inn is the food-led inn. These, quite simply, draw custom because of their food which will be available either thirteen or fourteen sessions per week. They often have a small separate restaurant area, and 60 per cent or more of their business will come from food sales, an adequate catering kitchen being essential. The menu is usually varied,

Figure 3.3

good value for money and includes a number of interesting or unusual dishes.

Many food-led inns are free houses but companies such as Woodhouse Inns (Hall and Woodhouse Ltd) and the ex-Country Style Inns (now part of the Old English Pub Company) have many excellent examples of this style of outlet.

The young person's pub

This is one of the most profitable segments of the pub business but also the most expensive in terms of investment in the property. The 1990s have seen the national development of Yates's Wine Bars, Firkin pubs and brands such as Rat and Parrot. These are developed much like film sets so that they can be easily (but expensively) changed as the fashion changes. They are often very large with trading areas as much as ten times greater than an average pub. It is commonplace to have average takings of over £5,000 a day in this style of outlet and many will be making profits of £1,000 per day. This sounds like a licence to print money and would be if it were not for the impact of the initial development costs and the heavy burden of regular refurbishment.

Figure 3.4

There are still a number of smaller privately run young person's pubs which rely on their atmosphere, clever lighting and the quality of their music to keep their customers loyal. Music has to be exactly right and it is this that catches out the ageing trendies who still believe they understand what their eighteen- to twenty-four-year old customers are currently enjoying.

These pubs tend to have a 'Jekyll and Hyde' nature as they cater for business people and shoppers during the day and early evening, thus generating good food sales and then concentrate on their main target group from 9 pm onwards.

At 9 pm the music style changes, its volume increases and the lighting is dimmed thus repelling the more mature customers and leaving space for their younger target market.

Premium draught and bottled lagers are a vital part of the sales mix, with smooth flow taking market share from the few cask conditioned ales that they stock. White wines, white spirits and soft drinks make up the bulk of the range.

In Figure 3.4 we illustrate this style of outlet with a pub of the 1980s as it shows the fickleness of the young persons' market. A 1980s Game Bird quickly becomes a 1990s White Elephant!

The town centre boozer

These were numerous until recently. They cater for hard drinking customers in town centres. They are usually down-market, male-dominated pubs selling keg beer and standard lager. Very little food is on offer or demanded. Prices tend to be low. There is a living to be made in this type of pub, but only just and they are certainly not to everyone's taste!

Wetherspoons pubs with their low pricing policy have picked up a lot of the daytime trade and consequently the town centre boozer has lost much of its market. Some have been converted into Scruffy Murphys mainly by adding copious quantities of Irish bric-a-brac and this has brought them into the more profitable young person's market.

Assessing the market

You have now decided the type of pub you want to run and the style of operation in which you are most likely to be successful. During the seventies and eighties, pubs were mainly profitable and consequently in short supply. Currently there are sufficient

Figure 3.5

pubs on the market and you will have a reasonable selection to choose from. This makes your assessment of the market even more important. Once you have chosen your type of pub, you must quickly start your research and expect it to be time-absorbing and very hard work.

You have a limited time to reach your conclusions and your research must be both relevant and practical. You need to sort out the 'nice to know' from the 'need to know'. There is much vital information that you need to acquire and a systematic and disciplined approach is essential.

Build a knowledge of the area

If you are already familiar with the area where your potential business is situated, then a lot of the answers will come more easily. The questions still need to be asked because, even if you know the area well, you have probably not needed to look so objectively at it in the past. Drive around the area and walk it too. Look at lunchtime to see the traffic flows and the pedestrian count. Look early evening to see what time the offices finish for the day and see when the residents arrive home. Look at night and see if the area is closed and shuttered or light and vibrant. Observe what the local people do at the weekend. Look at the shops and supermarkets: when do they open and close? Are the walls and fences clean or are they covered in graffiti? Most important of all, see if the area 'feels' right to you. Is it threatening? Is it likely to be violent? Do youths move around in large groups on weekend evenings?

Ask yourself, would you live there and, if the answer is no, then look at another pub in another area.

Where will my customers come from?

You need to know who your likely customers are and where they will come from. What jobs do they have and what type of houses do they live in? Will they be in recently acquired homes and heavily mortgaged or will they be in rented or low-mortgage houses? Your chance of getting much business in the short term from the former is clearly not very high. Are there potential customers around at lunchtime and early evening or is the area purely residential?

Are the likely customers people that you will feel comfortable with? If not, then proceed no further.

Is the area growing?

Is the area a growth area or is it in decline? Enquire at the town hall about future developments and plans for the area. Are the shops all open and looking prosperous? Are there new supermarkets being constructed or are there closed businesses with boarded-up windows? Is the area likely to have new roads that will bypass it and will this help or hinder your potential trade?

Is the local industry in good shape?

Does the local economy depend on the local industry or do residents commute to the city? Is the local industry secure and likely to expand or hold its own over the next ten years or is it winding down? Are there new business parks being constructed? A conversation with the locals in one of the competing pubs will answer many of these questions.

An investment in demographic information

A demographic study of the area by post code can be purchased and will help you understand the nature of the area more thoroughly. Some of the major brewers have this information as part of their data bank and may, if you were going to purchase their products, give you a print-out. Information available includes population, age group, social class, income group and even what newspapers they read. It will also tell you whether they are above- or below-average drinkers or whether they eat out more than the national average. Obviously, your chances of developing a successful food-led business would be diminished if your target customers ate out much less frequently than average.

Assessing the competition

A landlady with twenty years' experience recently remarked 'there used to be plenty of trade to go around. You just opened your doors and in they came'. That is clearly no longer the case and successful pubs are doing well by taking business from other pubs. There is no longer 'plenty to go around'.

A detailed knowledge of what competitor pubs are offering and how successful they are is an essential part of your research. This is not a once-only operation before taking on your pub but a subject that needs constant updating.

Who will be my competitors?

As with all apparently easy questions, the answer is very difficult. The pub next door may be a competitor but not necessarily. The Beefeater down the road or the disco pub near the bypass or even the two-bar pub on the nearby estate could be a competitor. A competitor pub is one that is attracting or is capable of attracting your target custom.

If, for instance, you are expecting to operate a food-led inn then the Beefeater could be a competitor. It is likely that you could position your inn away from the professional but standardized Beefeater approach. You may even be pleased to see it there as it would confirm that the area is capable of sustaining a major food operation.

If the disco pub happened to be a seventeenth-century building with beams and inglenooks and it was just the current landlord who had taken it down the music route, then this could, in different hands, become a major competitor.

The estate pub, built in the seventies and situated in the centre of the estate, is unlikely to be a direct competitor even if the proprietor attempts to supply good food at reasonable prices.

Your competitors could be anywhere within a radius of ten minutes' drive from your intended inn. Ask questions, buy pub guides and drive around the area. Try and make visits to each of them ideally on a Thursday or Friday evening or over the weekend.

Check their operation, their prices, the quality of the service and what they are offering but, most important of all, check the customers. How many cars do they have and do they look like company cars? What age groups? Do they look like regulars? Do they sound and look pleased with the hospitality? Are people drinking lager or cask-conditioned ales? How are they dressed? You can learn a lot from what people are wearing.

A smart and trendy bar was set up in Oxford some years ago and it was decided, in order to help it build an upmarket image, that a 'no jeans' dress policy would be enforced. The whole policy had to be reversed when it was discovered that the target customers nearly all wore jeans and those who were not part of the target custom all dressed up in the evenings. An expensive and completely avoidable mistake!

Beware of undertrading pubs in good locations

Just like the disco pub in the wrong market, beware of pubs that are undertrading. Although you need to have confidence that you will become the best operator in the area, you must also be realistic. If a good operator took over a pub in your target area, could it be a threat to you? It is usually harder to cope with losing 10 per cent of your business to a new competitor than to build up your trade in the first place.

Be objective

Always try to be objective about your competitors. There is a danger in being over-confident of your own abilities and dismissive of your competitors. It is easy for a professional to pick fault with most operations but remember, customers are not looking at the pub in the same kind of way. They are clearly there to enjoy food and drink in congenial company in surroundings that they feel comfortable in. They are not trying to pick fault as this would sour their enjoyment. Try to look through a customer's eyes so that your research can be truly objective.

Trade forecasts

Often all the information that you can obtain on a pub is its barrellage. This is especially true of tenancies and leases.

What is barrellage?

Beer barrellage includes draught and bottled ales and lagers. Excluding food, beer barrellage accounts for between 55 and 85 per cent of total wet trade with the balance being taken up by wines, spirits and soft drinks. The estate local is likely to be at the top of the range with the food-led inn nearer 55 per cent.

South of Birmingham, the average country pub excluding the larger brewery-managed houses will be selling around 200 beer barrels a year. Unless there is also a major food potential, it is unlikely anyone can get much of a living under this figure. As it is also the average, it underlines how many licensees are just scraping a living.

For the heavier drinking Midlands and North the average barrellage will be higher but volumes are falling and are nowhere near the levels when heavy industry was flourishing.

Note that in this context a barrel is thirty-six gallons of beer.

Look at the history of the pub

If you can get a look at the trade history of a pub, then this will tell you much about its potential. Some brewers are organized enough to go back twenty years but all should let you have five years' trade figures.

If, for instance, a pub has had five licensees over the last twenty years but the trade has never exceeded 150 barrels, ask yourself why will you do any better? Unless your answer is very convincing, as often with food potential it can be, then walk away and look for better opportunities.

Become a private eye

Ask questions of the old boy sitting in the corner. Just like the TV private eyes, you can get lots of information for the price of a drink. A helpful clue would be 'they haven't had a decent landlord since 1975'. At least, you might feel that you could buck the trend.

Always take a cautious view

It is all too easy to expect to double the trade. It can be done and regularly is done but it is not easy. Take a cautious view and, if the figures still make it possible for you to proceed, then it is likely that you will have a success on your hands.

Financial forecasts

It is essential before taking over a pub that you attempt as accurately as possible to forecast takings and profits, ideally over the first three years.

Seek expert help

There are specialists in this field but they are not easy to find. Ask around in the trade and work on recommendation only. If you over-estimate your potential profits, you may well not survive in your chosen business.

Converting barrellage to cash takings

You will remember from the paragraph on barrellage that the percentage of beer in the sales mix varies from one type of pub to another. If you decide, say, that a maximum of 60 per cent of trade (excluding food) is coming from beer sales, then on a 200 barrel pub the figures could look like this: 200 barrels at an average price per pint of, say, £1.80 equals 200 × 288 pints × £1.80 = £103,680 which equals 60 per cent of the wet trade. Then 100 per cent of the wet trade will be £103,680 ÷ 60 × 100 = £172,800. Deduct VAT of £25,736 and this leaves a rough estimate of net wet takings of £147,064.

You then need to sit and watch over a few trading sessions and try to make some estimates of actual takings. Try to decide what the take is on a very poor session, say Monday lunchtime, a poor session, say Tuesday night, an average session, say Wednesday evening and a good session, say Sunday lunchtime and a very good session, say Friday night. You could then start to build a trade pattern as shown in Figure 3.6.

If, after your observation, you took a very poor session to be £100, a poor session £125, an average session £175, a good session £250 and a very good session £325, your chart would be built up as in Figure 3.7.

This equates to an annual turnover excluding VAT of £143,830 and is close enough to your estimate of £147,064 to give you some confidence in your figures. Remember, be cautious and use the lower figure, perhaps rounding it down to £140,000.

	Morning	Afternoon	Evening
Monday	Very poor	Closed	Poor
Tuesday	Poor	Closed	Poor
Wednesday	Poor	Closed	Average
Thursday	Good	Very poor	Good
Friday	Very good	Very poor	Very Good
Saturday	Good	Average	Very Good
Sunday	Good	Closed	Poor

Figure 3.6 Building a trade pattern

A similar observation exercise can take place to establish the food take. Use the same chart system, count the number of meals served on the sessions you are watching and multiply by the average menu price.

Remember to deduct the VAT before calculating the annual turnover.

	Morning	Afternoon	Evening
Monday	100	Closed	125
Tuesday	125	Closed	125
Wednesday	125	Closed	175
Thursday	250	100	250
Friday	325	100	325
Saturday	250	175	325
Sunday	250	Closed	125
Totals	1425	375	1450

Figure 3.7 Putting values to the trade pattern

Assessing the gross profit percentage

Gross profit is calculated by taking the difference between the buying and selling price and expressing it as a percentage of the selling price. For example, you buy a bottle of wine for £2 and sell it for £4, then this equals 50 per cent gross profit (excluding VAT from both transactions).

Gross profit percentages on drinks vary considerably across the country with 55 to 60 per cent quite common in London and the Home Counties but down to 40 per cent in other parts of the country.

You cannot afford to be seriously out of line with competitor pubs on pricing, and efficiency is vital. Stock control is covered fully in Chapter 7.

To assess gross profit quickly, ask a genuine friend running a pub what he is achieving and, using his prices as the benchmark, estimate up or down.

Assessing the outgoings

You will have been given or you can obtain from your district council the business rate of the pub. Some pubs will be benefiting from interim relief but as a rule you just multiply the business rate value by the rate in the pound, i.e. business rate £22,500, rate in the pound £0.465, rates payable £10,462. Water costs are significant, especially if on a meter, so try to get a good idea of the figure from the existing licensee or your local water company. Rent will be a major expense in a tenanted or leased pub. Insurances are also significant, for the property, the contents, the licence, plus employer's and third party liability.

Wages and labour charge

Labour may be your biggest single expense and this varies as a percentage of takings from as little as 6 per cent in an estate local to as much as 20 per cent in a food-led traditional inn. These exclude the landlord and landlady who hopefully get paid from profits. A more accurate way of assessing labour is to use a chart as for takings. Work out for each session how many staff and how many hours. Decide on cleaning, is it two hours a morning or do you want an afternoon clean as well and then add those to the hours needed. Multiply the total hours by the current rate being paid locally and add on 10 per cent for National Insurance. You may wish to add in an annual £2,000 to ensure that you get an adequate holiday relief.

Energy

Heating and lighting are expensive items in pubs and inns. In a medium sized pub these could be around £5,000, more if your heating system or insulation is inefficient.

Other costs

The principle other costs are hygiene, covering everything from cleaning materials to laundry; promotions and advertising; minor repairs to the property and inventory; telephone; and transport and general sundries. In a well-ordered pub these should not exceed 5 per cent of your total takings.

Depreciation

The Inland Revenue currently allow you to depreciate your inventory and equipment at the rate of 25 per cent per year (capital allowances). Make sure that you do not just take the tax saving, but, if your finances allow, put the depreciation money into a separate, interest-earning account, so that you can renew your inventory when it becomes necessary.

Cost of ingoings when leasing or renting a pub

When taking over a pub, you will be faced with 'ingoings', the trade word for the money that you need to pay over to secure the business. It covers the following.

Trade inventory

Everything in the way of fixtures and fittings that is integral to the business is included from bar furniture to beer engines, from extractor fan to microwave oven and from lamp bulbs to a lavatory brush, all listed and valued by a licensed house valuer whom you will be paying to act on your behalf.

There are often 'optional items' on an inventory that are not really part of the business such as bedroom carpets that are valued and you can choose whether to buy or reject.

The value of the inventory is agreed in advance of the takeover day by both the outgoer's and the incomer's valuers.

Stock

These are goods for resale such as beer, wines, spirits and soft drinks. These are known as wet stock and cigarettes, crisps and nuts are generally included in this figure. Food, known as dry stock, is also counted and valued on the takeover day.

A stocktaker will be working on your behalf but probably appointed by your licensed house valuer.

Glasses, cutlery and crockery will also be counted and valued, as will goods not for resale such as logs, cleaning materials and bags of coal.

Remember to brief your stocktaker to reject any out of date wet or food stock. Sometimes stocktakers are not as sharp as they could be on this but it is your money, not theirs, that is being wasted.

Deposit

The third major part of ingoings is the deposit. It varies in size but is usually a significant sum, perhaps equivalent to three months' rent or four weeks' supplies. Interest is paid and, as long as accounts are settled in full, the deposit is returned at the termination of the tenancy.

Legal costs on leases

It is usual, when brewery companies grant new leases, that lessees (tenants) are responsible for both their own and the brewery's legal costs. For a straightforward lease with no complications, this is likely to cost the lessee around £1,000 in total.

Costs of a valuer

The final part of ingoings is the cost of the valuer. This is based on a percentage of the value of the inventory and stock: £1,000 or more is usually required.

Working capital

Inventory, stock, deposit and fees make up the ingoings but allowance must be made for working capital. Although working capital should be kept to a minimum in any business, it would be difficult to operate without the equivalent of two weeks' expected purchases.

Total cost of ingoings

A small tenancy's ingoings could be as little as £10,000 but a large tenancy or lease may well be six or seven times as much. On leases, you also need to remember that you will be responsible for putting the pub in good repair.

Cost of ingoings when buying a free house

The trade inventory is often, but not always, included in the sale price and it is essential that you confirm this when making your offer. There will be no deposit but legal and financial costs will be higher than those already described.

Cash flow analysis

You know how much you are likely to take and make from your pub. You know the costs of taking over the business but you now need to assess if you will have sufficient cash at the right time to allow you to proceed.

When a small business fails, it is often because it was underfunded in the first place. It is not only the initial capital you need but the cash generated by the business on a daily and weekly basis which enables you to pay your bills and buy your goods for resale.

Your takings will vary, perhaps according to season; you will be paying some bills weekly, some monthly and a few annually.

Cash flow management is all about having the right amount of money available in the right place and at the right time.

Identifying pressure points

Even the most modest businesses need to plan their cash flow on a weekly, monthly and annual basis. Demands for money arise and it is essential that you try and identify the times of the year when your cash resources will be at a low ebb. Banks are usually more helpful if you approach them for overdrafts in advance of needing the money. It would impress the manager even more if you negotiated an overdraft for January and February whilst your takings were buoyant in July or August.

A cash business such as a pub has the advantage of having its customers pay for their food and drink on a daily basis whereas most bills will need to be settled weekly or monthly.

Don't forget the VAT

VAT is a problem and a blessing. You collect VAT from your customers every day but can hang on to it for up to four months as VAT bills are settled quarterly, one month in arrears. You should prudently set aside the VAT element of your sales in a separate interest-earning deposit account and ensure that the money is there when needed.

You may wish to pay your VAT monthly to remove the worry of a big bill at the end of the quarter and Customs and Excise allow you to do this.

Do not forget that, if you ring through your till £1175, only £1,000 of it is yours at the current rate of 17.5 per cent and the rest goes to Customs and Excise as VAT after you have deducted the VAT you have paid out.

Completing the business plan

Who needs the plan?

Clearly, you do, because it is the chart by which you will steer your business.

The bank or other financial institution from which you are raising capital will need to be convinced that you have a viable business opportunity. There is no better way of persuading a financier than by putting compelling facts and figures in front of him or her.

If you are renting or leasing the pub from a brewer or pub operator, the management of that company will be interviewing you to judge whether you are the best person to take over the business. You may be in competition with several other hopefuls, particularly if it is an attractive pub proposition.

Your business plan, lucidly presented, will have a major influence on the final outcome. If your plan is not thought through or is unconvincing, then your application, quite rightly, will be rejected. In producing your plan, you may well have to balance conflicting factors. Assuming you are to some degree changing the direction of the business, you have to decide on the pace of change.

For example, if you have a two-bar pub that you wish to convert to one bar with a heavy emphasis on food, the consequence would be that you lose the pool players and maybe the darts players as well. You may also have to spend six weeks and £20,000 creating a suitable catering kitchen. In these circumstances, there is no point in killing off your games area on day one; you will need that custom to tide you over until you are ready to launch the new style of business.

You may, however, take an opposite view and decide that the custom the pub already has plays no part in the future pub and that it will be better to close the pub, do all the necessary work to change its direction and reopen with a bang with the new-look operation. In this case, you will be building your customer base from scratch.

The decision between continuity and a clean break will be yours but it is a fundamental one and it must be fully thought through as part of your business plan.

'I'll wait and see what the customers want'

This strategy is no good – you must be the one who drives your business forward; you cannot afford to chop and change it on the whim of one or two customers. The customers are the most important people in the pub but you must set out your stall to attract the customers who will enjoy the style, the atmosphere and food and drink that you will be offering.

A clear action plan for your business

Your business plan must be clear and logical and lead to a sustainable and ultimately profitable future. It will need to be adapted over time as circumstances change but, if the basics are right, then refining and building on your plan will lead to more success.

Facts as well as figures

All the work that you have done whilst assessing the opportunity will be built into your business plan. Because you need to convince people, not only about the figures and the pub but about yourself, the plan should also include a description of yourself, your partner if appropriate, your age, education, achievements, employment and, most importantly, your trade or business experience.

Other elements should include:

- a description of the pub, its site and location;
- the competition;
- a SWOT (strengths, weaknesses, opportunities, threats) analysis. (As part of your assessment process, look at all the above in connection with the pub you are applying for. It's a sure way of spotting a problem if you find the weaknesses far outweigh the strengths or if the opportunities are heavily outnumbered by the threats. It's very simple and very effective.);
- your target market;
- your marketing plans;
- short- and medium-term plans for upgrading the building;
- the operation and how you will manage it;
- the one-year plan and cash flow;
- the three-year plan and cash flow.

Yes, a three-year plan! You probably thought that forecasting one week's trade was hard enough and one year more than sufficient. But a three-year plan is really a minimum requirement for a successful business. Like all plans, it can be adapted to meet changing circumstances but a good, honest attempt to forecast takings and expenses trends is essential.

You will see that four financial schedules are included in a thorough business plan. In the displayed examples there are:

Profit & Loss forecast		Year 1 £	Year 1 %	Year 2 £	Year 2 %	Year 3 £	Year 3 %
Takings	Wet	170,000	89	195,000	88	215,000	87
	Catering	20,000	10	25,000	11	30,000	12
	Vending M/c	1,000	1	1,000	0	1,000	0
	Total	191,000	100	221,000	100	246,000	100
Gross profit	Wet	86,700		97,500		107,500	
	Catering	9,500		12,500		15,750	
	Other	1,000		1,000		1,000	
	Total	97,200	51	111,000	50	124,250	51
Labour	Relief	(2,000)		(2,000)		(2,000)	
	Wages	(11,461)	–6	(15,470)	–7	(17,220)	–7
	Contract labour	(440)		(440)		(440)	
	ERNI	(914)		(1,234)		(1,374)	
	Pensions	(1,912)		(2,581)		(2,873)	
	Total	(16,727)	–9	(21,725)	–10	(23,907)	–10
Energy	Electricity	(3,000)		(3,150)		(3,308)	
	Gas	(1,000)		(1,050)		(1,103)	
	Other fuel	(500)		(500)		(500)	
	Total	(4,500)	–2	(4,700)	–2	(4,911)	–2

General Expenses	Music/Ent.	(1,196)		(1,196)		(1,196)	
	Utensils	(752)		(752)		(752)	
	Hygiene	(1,000)		(1,050)		(1,103)	
	Telephone	(600)		(600)		(600)	
	Repairs	(1,100)		(1,100)		(1,100)	
	Redecoration	(7,500)		(3,000)		(3,000)	
	Transport	(520)		(1,040)		(1,040)	
	Bar sundries	(260)		(390)		(390)	
	Hse promotion	(752)		(1,000)		(1,000)	
	Sundries	(1,496)		(1,800)		(1,800)	
	Total	(15,176)	–8	(11,928)	–5	(11,981)	–5
Controllable Profit		60,796	32	72,647	33	83,451	34
	Rent & rates	(31,200)		(31,200)		(31,200)	
	Bank fees	(2,160)		(1,080)		(1,080)	
	Prof. fees	(2,160)		(2,160)		(2,160)	
	Depreciation	(3,500)		(3,500)		(3,500)	
	Licences	(300)		(300)		(300)	
	Insurance	(1,200)		(1,200)		(1,200)	
	Total	(40,520)	–21	(39,440)	–18	(39,440)	–16
Net profit		20,277	11	33,207	15	44,011	18
Gross profit percentages	Wet	51.00%		50.00%		50.00%	
	Catering	47.50%		50.00%		52.50%	

Figure 3.8 A three-year profit forecast

Cash flow forecast	Year 1	Year 2	Year 3
Income	224,426	259,675	289,050
Output tax (VAT)	(25,403)	(37,415)	(42,000)
Stock purchases	(95,134)	(109,466)	(121,515)
Net wages	(8,648)	(11,674)	(12,994)
Contract labour	(440)	(440)	(440)
ERNI	(3,266)	(4,409)	(4,908)
Pensions	(1,912)	(2,581)	(2,873)
Energy	(3,950)	(4,675)	(4,885)
General expenses	(14,873)	(11,772)	(11,979)
Rent & rates	(31,200)	(31,200)	(31,200)
Bank fees	(2,160)	(1,080)	(1,080)
Professional fees	(3,660)	(2,160)	(2,160)
Licences	(300)	(300)	(300)
Insurance	(1,200)	(1,200)	(1,200)
Input tax recovery (VAT)	17,872	24,823	26,812
Input tax (VAT)	(22,132)	(25,387)	(27,146)
Inventory	(15,000)	0	0
Deposit	(6,000)	0	0
Renewals (Capex)	(5,000)	(1,500)	(2,000)
Living expenses	(5,200)	(5,200)	(5,200)
Annual	(3,181)	34,039	43,982
Cumulative	(3,181)	30,858	74,840
Funding	30,000		
Revised cumulative	26,819	60,858	104,840

Figure 3.9 A three-year cash flow forecast

- a three-year profit and loss account (Figure 3.8);
- a three-year cash flow projection (Figure 3.9);
- a detailed one-year profit and loss account (Figure 3.10);
- a detailed first-year cash flow (Figure 3.11).

Cash flow measures the cash coming into and going out of your business. It is quite possible to have a profitable business but actually to run out of cash. You can decide from this the pace at which, for example, you carry out improvements to or decorate the premises so that you ensure that you do not get into financial difficulties.

Remember that the formation of the plan will have involved you in many hours of work and probably some expenditure as well. You have, though, not risked your capital until you have signed on the dotted line.

However much work has been involved, if you feel uncomfortable with your business plan or think it too risky or too optimistic, then abort the project. You can make a good living from a pub but you can also lose money. If in doubt, walk away.

It takes courage but do it.

Summary

- only choose a pub in which you feel temperamentally comfortable;
- location, location, location;
- recognize your pub type;
- assess the market and the area;
- assess the competition – be objective;
- trade forecasts – be realistic;
- financial forecasts – be cautious;
- remember cash flow is the lifeblood of your business;
- a clear action plan for your business;
- if in doubt, walk away!

Profit and loss forecast		May	June	July	March	April	Total
Takings	Wet	13,600	13,600	15,300	13,600	13,600	170,000
	Catering	1,600	1,600	1,800	1,600	1,600	20,000
	Vending M/c	80	80	90	80	80	1,000
	Total	15,280	15,280	17,190	15,280	15,280	191,00
Gross profit	Wet	6,936	6,936	7,803	6,936	6,936	86,700
	Catering	760	760	855	760	760	9,500
	Other	80	80	90	80	800	1,00
	Total	7,776	7,776	8,748	7,776	7,776	97,200
Labour	Relief						(2,000)
	Wages	(917)	(917)	(1,031)	(917)	(917)	(11,461)
	Contract labour	(100)	(80)	(80)			(440)
	ERNI	(73)	(73)	(82)	(73)	(73)	(914)
	Pensions	(153)	(153)	(172)	(153)	(153)	(1,912)
	Total	(1,243)	(1,223)	(1,365)	(1,143)	(1,143)	(16,727)
Energy	Electricity	(210)	(150)	(150)	(330)	(240)	(3,000)
	Gas	(70)	(50)	(50)	(110)	(80)	(1,000)
	Other fuel	(35)	(25)	(25)	(55)	(40)	(500)
	Total	(315)	(225)	(225)	(495)	(360)	(4,500)

General Expenses	Music/Ent.	(115)	(92)	(92)	(92)	(92)	(1,196)
	Utensils	(72)	(58)	(58)	(58)	(58)	(752)
	Hygiene	(96)	(77)	(77)	(77)	(77)	(1,000)
	Telephone	(58)	(46)	(46)	(46)	(46)	(600)
	Repairs		(100)	(100)	(100)	(100)	(1,100)
	Redecoration	(1,500)	(1,500)	(1,125)			(7,500)
	Transport	(50)	(40)	(40)	(40)	(40)	(520)
	Bar sundries	(25)	(20)	(20)	(20)	(20)	(260)
	Hse promotion	(72)	(58)	(58)	(58)	(58)	(752)
	Sundries	(144)	(115)	(115)	(115)	(115)	(1,496)
	Total	(2,132)	(2,106)	(1,731	(606)	(606)	(15,176)
Controllable Profit		4,086	4,222	5,427	5,532	5,667	60,797
	Rent & rates	(3,000)	(2,400)	(2,400)	(2,400)	(2,400)	(31,200)
	Bank fees	(180)	(180)	(180)	(180)	(180)	(2,160)
	Prof. fees	(180)	(180)	(180)	(180)	(180)	(2,160)
	Depreciation	(337)	(269)	(269)	(337)	(269)	(3,500)
	Licences	(25)	(25)	(25)	(25)	(25)	(300)
	Insurance	(100)	(100)	(100)	(100)	(100)	(1,200)
	Total	(3,822)	(3,154)	(3,154)	(3,154)	(3,154)	(40,520)
Net profit		264	1,068	2,273	2,378	2,513	20,277
Gross profit	Wet	51.00%	51.00%	51.00%	51.00%	51.00%	51.00%
	Catering	47.50%	47.50%	47.50%	47.50%	47.50%	47.50%

Figure 3.10 A detailed one-year profit forecast

Cash flow forecast	April	May	June	July	August	September
Income		17,954	17,954	20,198	24,687	20,198
Output tax (VAT)					(8,356)	
Stock purchases	(3,000)	(5,838)	(7,504)	(8,234)	(9,902)	(8,859)
Net wages		(530)	(706)	(772)	(927)	(838)
Contract labour		(100)	(80)	(80)	(100)	(80)
ERNI			(284)	(284)	(319)	(391)
Pensions		(153)	(153)	(172)	(210)	(172)
Energy		(35)	(235)	(175)	(345)	(185)
General expenses		(1,066)	(2,119)	(1,919)	(1,794)	(1,794)
Rent & rates		(3,000)	(2,400)	(2,400)	(3,000)	(2,400)
Bank fees				(540)		
Professional fees	(1,500)	(180)	(180)	(180)	(180)	(180)
Licences		(300)				
Insurance		(100)	(100)	(100)	(100)	(100)
Input tax recovery (VAT)		0	0	0	8,336	0
Input tax (VAT)	(3,413)	(1,462)	(1,646)	(1,815)	(1,917)	(1,698)
Inventory	(15,000)					
Deposit	(6,000)					
Renewals (capital)			(2,500)	(1,000)	(1,000)	(500)
Living expenses	(400)	(400)	(400)	(400)	(400)	(400)
Monthly	(29,313)	4,790	(353)	2,128	4,474	2,601
Cumulative	(29,313)	(24,523)	(24,876)	(22,748)	(18,274)	(15,673)
Funding	30,000					
Revised cumulative	687	5,477	5,124	7,252	11,726	14,327

Figure 3.11 A detailed one-year cash flow forecast

October	November	December	January	February	March	April
15,710	17,954	22,443	13,466	17,954	17,954	17,954
	(9,025)			(8,022)		
(6,983)	(7,296)	(8,964)	(6,461)	(7,088)	(7,504)	(7,504)
(662)	(684)	(838)	(618)	(662)	(706)	(706)
0	0	0	0	0	0	0
(319)	(248)	(284)	(356)	(213)	(284)	(284)
(134)	(153)	(191)	(115)	(153)	(153)	(153)
(250)	(485)	(325)	(390)	(740)	(415)	(370)
(1,731)	(1,232)	(669)	(606)	(669)	(669)	(606)
(2,400)	(3,000)	(2,400)	(2,400)	(3,000)	(2,400)	(2,400)
(540)			(540)			(540)
(180)	(180)	(180)	(180)	(180)	(180)	(180)
(100)	(100)	(100)	(100)	(100)	(100)	(100)
0	5,178	0	0	4,358	0	0
(1,563)	(1,419)	(1,610)	(1,257)	(1,392)	(1,392)	(1,476)
(400)	(400)	(400)	(400)	(400)	(400)	(400)
449	(1,162)	6,482	43	(307)	3,751	3,235
(15,224)	(16,386)	(9,903)	(9,860)	(10,167)	(6,416)	(3,181)
14,776	13,614	20,097	20,140	19,833	23,584	26,819

Figure 3.11 (*continued*)

4 Setting out your stall

One of the answers often given by applicants for pubs is 'We'll see what the customers want'. This may sound responsive to customer needs and therefore very enlightened, but the problem with this type of thinking is that it ignores the bigger question: 'who are my target customers?'

If, as part of your plan for the inn, you decide that the pool table must go, it is very little use asking the pool team what they think of the idea. Conversely, if you decide to put a pool table in an area previously used as a restaurant, you are not likely to get much encouragement for this change from the diners (see Figure 4.1). You must decide what style of operation you intend and then set out your stall.

In this chapter, we are going to cover the setting up of your business, mainly from a marketing rather than an operational view point. From the various types of pubs and inns such as 'the estate local' and 'the young persons' pub', we have chosen just two as examples to cover in more depth: the traditional inn (food-led) and the general local. We picked these because the traditional food-led inn is the most difficult style of operation to run well and because there are, by far, more general locals around the country than any other pub type.

We will highlight for each group:

- the core custom;
- the main purpose of the customer's visit;
- service and style;

Figure 4.1

- products on offer and not on offer;
- facilities;
- decor, lighting and furnishings;
- identity, signage and advertising;

and, in the traditional inn in particular, we will list the things that you should NOT find.

The traditional inn (food-led)

This will be in a rural and attractive location. The building will seem to have heritage, will always have a good car park and will usually have a well-kept garden. Although there are exceptions to every rule, you will not be able to make this style of operation work in a town or city, however attractive the building is.

Core custom

Its main customer group will be those aged over 50. These may come as couples or in small groups. Women in groups of two, three or four will be strongly represented, especially at lunchtime. This particular market segment is growing fast and, with the post-war baby boom, it will continue to do so for several years to come. The customers are drawn mainly from the A, B and C1 social groups which means they have professional, managerial or supervisory backgrounds. They are comfortably off and although not free spenders, they do eat out regularly, seeking out value for money. You are unlikely to see many of this group arriving after nine o'clock in the evening.

The second group will be business people who will have driven for up to fifteen minutes to get there. These will not be restricted to a one-hour lunch break and the pace of the meal can be relaxed, as long as it is efficient. This group is trading down from smart restaurants that did so well in the eighties when expense account spending was buoyant. They are looking for value for money, atmosphere and interesting, perhaps unusual, dishes.

The third, but miscellaneous, group will be two sets of ramblers. The first, complete with their Ordnance Survey maps and walking boots, the second in their cars and clutching their pub guide. There will also be the 'event' people attending a local christening or the opening of a nearby garden.

The main purpose of the customer's visit

The clear and main reason for visiting a food-led traditional inn will be to eat. Obvious in a way but it is essential to have this clearly in your mind when planning your operation. Once you are established, at least 60 per cent of your turnover will come from food and at least 80 per cent from food and the drinks served with it. Food preparation and food service will therefore dominate your operation.

You will get the occasional customers popping in for a drink but they will have to fit in with the eaters and not the other way around. If you are going to get £50 from a table and four chairs by selling meals, it cannot be in your interests to allow the table to be used by a drinker spending £5 over the same period. You will be able to accommodate a few local drinkers more easily after about half past nine when many of your diners will have completed their meals and will be on their way home.

Style

Food-led traditional inns operate most successfully without a formal restaurant. Service levels expected in restaurants are costly to maintain and invariably mean prices beyond the level that is acceptable to the core custom. They do work and we can all point out highly successful pub-restaurants but there are many more failures than success stories.

The classic food-led inn will serve food thirteen or fourteen sessions per week. It will have a menu of around twelve main dishes, six starters and a selection of puddings. These will, in the main, be prepared on the premises. The menu will usually change by season but maybe half of the favourite dishes will be retained. In addition, there will be a few 'specials' of the day, freshly prepared from fresh ingredients and usually chalked up neatly on a blackboard.

'Freshly prepared on the premises' is an important part of your consumer proposition as this gives the individualism that the core market is seeking. This is labour-intensive but, assuming you buy well and use seasonal ingredients, the gross profit will be high. You need to get turnover to a level that will allow you to employ kitchen help because this type of food preparation and service is extremely hard work and you will need to get a break from it at least once a week to avoid burning yourself out within a year or two. Food can be bought in from manufacturers, microwaved and garnished and served to the customers. Although this is very much easier, it has two major disadvantages. It is difficult to get a satisfactory level of gross profit without over-pricing the meals and, however well you dress it up, your customers will know its origins and will not become regulars. We will be covering the subject of gross profit more fully in Chapter 7.

Customers will be eating throughout the premises and, when weather permits, on the patio and nearby garden as well. If your garden is large, take care not to get trapped into having your waiting staff wandering around the grounds looking for some distant customer. Make the rule that meals can only be served into a clearly-defined outside area.

The style of the operation needs to be informal, relaxed but efficient. Dress should be equally informal: smart but casual with staff wearing clothes that they feel good in.

One of the worst methods of identifying customers who have ordered food is the use of cloakroom tickets. Calling out the numbers tends to sound like summoning boats in on a municipal boating lake. It is much more friendly to get a name and even better to get a name and where the customer will be sitting.

Everything about the place must be clean and tidy. The lawn neatly trimmed, the windows regularly cleaned and the wood and brass polished. Menus, if you are using them, must be fresh and clean and blackboard chalking must be neat with lettering that can be read without difficulty, especially by the over-fifties. Scrawly writing in red and green chalk may seem pretty to the writer but is usually much more difficult to read than neatly printed lettering in white.

Music or sometimes the lack of it is a vital ingredient in any style of licensed outlet. In a food-led traditional inn, it is equally important. The food could be right, the lighting superb and the furnishings completely to your taste but, if heavy metal music is blaring out of the speakers, the whole ambience of the place will be spoilt. Music in all inns and pubs should always be played through high-quality equipment with sufficient speakers to control volume. Six speakers throughout a room, with individual volume control, will be much better than one, when the music will be too loud for those sitting near it and too quiet at the far side of the room.

Play music that will be to the taste of your main target group. It could be popular classical or film themes or even tuneful music from the fifties and sixties. Equally, you could decide that there will be no music. Very much better to have no music than poor-quality sound.

Service

Service needs to be relaxed but efficient but, in food-led traditional inns and all other types of licensed bars, customers must be acknowledged quickly when they reach the bar. Customers in the main are not unreasonable people; they will wait patiently if you are busy serving; what they do insist on, however, is recognition. A smile, an 'I'll be with you in a moment', a brief nod, some eye contact or anything to tell the customer that his presence has been noted is all that is necessary. But you have very little time to do it, just ten seconds.

Make the ten-second rule the cornerstone of your customer service and you can be guaranteed that your business will improve. Try it yourself and, if your experience is similar to our own, you will find that around 80 per cent of establishments will fail.

Try to find the opportunity to check with your customers during their meal if everything is all right. Try to keep the approach fresh and avoid asking questions 'parrot fashion'. When the customers start to leave after their meal, make sure that you and your staff make a point of thanking them for their custom; 'Thanks very much, see you again' and other similar phrases are all that is required.

When you are talking with customers at their table, try and physically get down to their level. It is one of the lessons that we are slow to learn from America but it helps the customer to feel in control and therefore comfortable and relaxed.

We will be covering recruitment in Chapter 6 but, as part of your service style, encourage staff to smile a lot. Smiling staff do wonders for your business. It is an old saying and somewhat trite but if you want your staff to smile a lot, employ staff who smile a lot. If they look miserable at the interview, blame yourself, not them, when they look miserable behind your bar.

Remember that 'Smiling Service Sells'.

Offer credit facilities

When customers are first at the bar and are clearly going to eat, try to get a name and start a tab running. There is no doubt that you are likely to sell more drinks, puddings and coffees if the customer does not have to continually have his hand in his pocket. Although it is going to cost you anything from 3 per cent of the final bill, it is worth taking major credit cards. This again will encourage extra sales and allow the meal cost to exceed the money in the customer's pocket, purse or wallet.

Continuity and reliability

Continuity and reliability are two essential words in successful innkeeping. It is better to serve moderate food with reasonable service than excellent food and service one day and poor standards the next. Customers do not easily forgive nasty surprises when they go out to eat. If they have a bad eating-out experience, they are likely to avoid that operation for months or even years rather than risk a repetition. Although the old saying states 'everyone is entitled to at least one off day', sadly, innkeepers cannot even afford that.

There is a Buckinghamshire country inn we know that is highly successful. The food is average but the service is good and the operation completely reliable. You always get what you expect and hence the inn continues to thrive. Service and product quality must be delivered day after day without fail. Just like the dairy farmer whose cows need milking twice every day, seven days a week, the innkeeper must always attend to 'doing the milking'.

Products

It is important to understand what products to feature in a traditional food-led inn. We have already described the style of the food operation and the other products need to be compatible with this.

The clue is in the title 'traditional' – traditional ales served in the traditional way through beer engines or straight from the cask. These are essential and the successful innkeeper stocks a choice of two or more different brews. The decision on the number of brands stocked will be dictated by speed of throughput and product quality. It is better to stock just one cask-conditioned bitter that is in peak condition because of rapid throughput rather than three that may hang around a week or more and lose their freshness. Too many innkeepers make the mistake of over-estimating the marketing benefits of a large number of different cask-conditioned bitters and forgetting product quality.

Do not stock brewery-conditioned ('keg') bitter unless it is impossible for you, because of poor cellar conditions, to stock 'real ale', otherwise definitely the wrong marketing message is sent to the discerning drinker.

Most pubs and inns need to stock at least two lagers and the traditional inn is no exception. If you have the choice, then go for one standard lager such as Carlsberg, Carling Black Label or Heineken and one premium such as Stella Artois, Holsten or Carlsberg Export. Avoid the over-priced Australian, American and Canadian lagers. These have their place in several types of pub but not your traditional inn.

Serve a range of white wines by the glass, perhaps as many as six. There are good wines available from around the world and your choice is wide. Seek out good value wines, recommended by your wine suppliers. Some wines from the better known regions tend to be pricey but there are excellent examples from the less fashionable growers.

Try to create a demand for two or three red wines by the glass. There is now such a huge range of decent quality wines at sensible prices that you could be spoilt for choice.

Learn about wines, try to get on a course sponsored by a wine supplier, and taste and experiment. Apart from being an agreeable occupation, you will also find wine sales increasing along with your growing confidence in the subject.

Do remember to serve good-quality wine and price it accordingly. You will find that, given the choice, a customer will prefer to pay £1.50 for a good glass of wine rather than £1 for a poor one.

Try to avoid serving your wines through optics and definitely give wine pumps a miss in this style of inn. Your only move towards modernity should be a counter-mounted cork pull. Customers like to hear corks pop!

A full range of spirits on optic is essential. Make sure you have a choice of whiskies, cognacs, gins, vodkas and rums. Perhaps specialize in a larger range of malt whiskies or brandies: these though should be served through thimble measures rather than by optic.

Among the things that you will NOT be serving are:

- bottled designer lagers served 'by the neck';
- cocktails except Pimms or Bloody Marys;
- super-strength ciders.

Care should be taken not to clutter up your backfitting with open boxes of crisps or cards of nuts. It is right to sell these but very much better to decant them into a suitable dish when serving them.

Decor, lighting and furnishings

We cover the physical side of furnishings in the next chapter but in this section we are trying to describe the 'feel' of the operation. When large pub companies decide to refurbish a bar, they get their designer to create a board with samples or pictures of the component parts such as carpets, curtains, style of seating, lighting and colour schemes. These have various names but we think of them as 'feely boards'. You should look at the interior of your inn as if it were a 'feely board'. What impression is it giving to your target market? Is it consistent? Is the lighting too dim, too bright or too uniform? What is the focal point, is it the bar, the fire or some other feature? Are the furnishings in keeping with the character of the building or are they just bland and mass-produced?

In a traditional inn, it is essential that the furnishings are in character. A few years ago, when visiting what was purported to be the oldest inn in Britain, it was deeply disappointing to find the furnishings and decor straight out of a late twentieth-century catalogue. Customers may not mention it but they will instinctively feel the place is a sham.

If there are old settles in your inn, then refurbish them and make them a core part of your furnishings. Make sure that all wood that needs polish is highly polished and all brass sparkling. Although tables must be practical, try to mix in some different shapes. Old chairs are more difficult as they tend to fall apart when introduced into a commercial environment. Do try, though, to get some variety.

It is tempting to cover the floor with fitted carpet but it can take from the ambience of an inn. Flagstone floors are cold in the winter but look terrific. Polished wood floors can be slippery but nothing looks better than a traditional floor with perhaps rugs or mats covering parts of it.

Changes in floor or ceiling levels can create interest as long as they look natural. A raised floor to facilitate a view from the window could improve the environment for customers. If it can be achieved at reasonable price, room shapes can be varied by a half-wall, a post or a screen. It needs to look as if it was always there; there is nothing worse than bits of a building that have no purpose, other than decor.

A mix of lighting sources, creating pools of light and shadow, is what you should try to achieve – not so dark as to have your customers struggling to identify what they are sticking their fork into or so bright as to make them feel like surgeons whilst dissecting their rare steak. Up- rather than down-pointing lighting tends to iron out the wrinkles and this is likely to make your fifty-plus target market feel and look more youthful. There is nothing like the 'feel good' factor to attract them back again to your inn.

Bric-a-brac is important in setting the scene. Avoid instant themeing. How many inns do you know where the owners have spent a week or two picking up two tons of rusty agricultural implements to hang on their walls? There is nothing wrong with having a theme but let it evolve slowly. Buy bits and pieces that you actually like the look of and find a suitable home for them in your bar.

Overall, the decor should be of natural and traditional materials with no hint of plastic or chrome. You can make a vast difference to the look and feel of your inn without spending too much money.

Take your time and proceed with great caution. Remember that your inn could have been there for up to 500 years and has slowly changed and evolved over all those years. Don't try to change it all in your first month!

Facilities and things to avoid

Most food-led traditional inns are one bar with perhaps a small restaurant area leading off it. There are a few where the public bar has been retained. In these, it is like running two different pubs under one roof.

Decent toilets are essential. They need to be clean, well ventilated and have hot and cold running water, soap, nailbrush and towel. If you are feeling extravagant, you may decide to supply both a towel and a blow hand drier. In the Ladies, you will need at least two cubicles and ideally two handbasins as well, a mirror with good lighting and a stool plus, as pleasant optional extras, some tissues, handcream and perhaps a small vase of flowers. Central heating or some form of heating is important.

One hears it said that customers choose pubs by the quality of their toilets. This is probably an over-statement but it is likely that they reject pubs by the poor quality of their toilets. Over-the-top decor in toilets is a bit of a gimmick but, as long as it does not cost too much and deprive other parts of the operation of cash, it is worth considering.

Clearly, pool tables have no place in the traditional food-led inn even if you have space available. Eating and pool just do not mix. To a lesser extent, darts boards are hard to justify.

There may be a call for darts from your locals later in the evening but it is probable that the space can be better utilized.

You might consider having a shove halfpenny board or table skittles available to bring out when space permits. These are traditional games and therefore compatible with your style of operation.

Juke boxes should never be installed in this style of pub. The music must be under the innkeeper's control and with a juke box it cannot be. The good news is it would not make any money anyway so you are not giving up a potential income stream.

A great deal of money is made from fruit machines (AWPs) but only in certain types of pub. They do not have a place in this type of operation for three main reasons:

- your target customers do not like them;
- you could use the space for a table and four chairs;
- a machine is unlikely to take enough money to cover its rent.

The same can be said for most video games with the possible exception of a quiz machine. But, for all types of electronic play equipment, the following applies:

- when in doubt, leave it out.

Accommodation

Many traditional inns have a few bedrooms which they let as an ancillary to the main parts of the business. Others are more seriously involved, where the letting of rooms represents an important contribution to total profits.

Before attempting to let rooms, the innkeeper has to understand the legal requirements, which are specific and must be observed (see 'Fire Precautions' and 'Innkeepers' in Chapter 11).

Over recent years, the inn has filled the gap in the market between the hotel with all its services and relatively high price and the bed and breakfast unlicensed guest house with few services and low price.

This section of the market has flourished because of the value for money it represents and the attraction the inn has for customers who want to enjoy an evening in convivial surroundings. The hotel may be too large and too formal, the guest house lacking a bar and too restrained.

It follows that, if you wish to enter this competitive market, you need to be able to offer a good friendly bar in the evening as well as an interesting choice of evening meals.

Increasingly, customers are seeking rooms which have their own bathroom and toilet ('en suite' facilities to use the jargon). Except at the lower end of the market, these are now almost obligatory.

Other attractions in letting rooms – tea- and coffee-making facilities, colour television – may also now be considered necessary but direct-line telephones, hair dryers and trouser presses are extras which most guests may not want, and therefore do not wish to (indirectly) pay for.

High standards of decoration, furnishings, heating and lighting to give an attractive and comfortable feel to the room are necessary if you are to build custom. The rooms need to be reasonably sound-insulated, especially if sited over the bar or kitchen.

Attention needs to be given not only to the basics, such as the comfort of the beds, but also details such as the height and size of the bathroom mirror (can both a five foot man and a six foot six man shave in it with equal ease?) and the positioning of mirrors and lighting in the bedroom (can a woman confidently make up her face in daylight and at night-time and can your guests read in bed without straining their eyes?).

Whether to equip rooms with twin beds or double beds is very much a matter of the type of customer you are attracting. You need to get the mix right to obtain the greatest use from your bedrooms.

However excellent the rooms, the business will not grow unless the warmth of welcome received by guests is of a high standard. All the best rules you apply to customer care in your bar or restaurant need to apply to overnight guests. They are spending a relatively large amount if they take dinner and patronize the bar as well as having bed and breakfast. They are also fine ambassadors for your inn if all sectors of the business have satisfied them.

There are, of course, some disadvantages to letting rooms:

- initial capital cost;
- loss of privacy and free time for the innkeepers – who rarely have the house to themselves;
- arrangements have to be made for guests booking in or out at awkward hours;
- not all guests will turn out to be well-behaved or fit in happily with you, your staff or customers;
- some guests will steal – or take 'souvenirs' of their stay;
- payment for rooms has to be properly controlled to avoid bounced cheques or other bad debts.

Nevertheless, letting rooms can be a profitable business:

- there is only minimal staff cost in cleaning rooms, making beds etc.;
- most of the room charge drops through to the bottom line.

Filling the rooms is the key factor. Large hotel chains agonize over their room occupancy rate – a shift of a few percentage points can alter the profit and loss account dramatically.

Finally, there is the question of what you charge for bed and breakfast. This is related, as always, to what the market will bear: it will reflect the quality of your rooms and the level of demand in your locality. Increasingly, it will be influenced by the competition from hotels which are more aware than they have ever been of offering more competitive prices. The hotel room tariff as published is surprisingly often open to negotiation.

The professional innkeeper will be confident that he or she can compete – there may not be a heated indoor pool, room service and night porter but there will be quality, value for money and an unmatched standard of personalized customer care.

Signs and advertising

External signs to a traditional food-led inn should be under- rather than over-stated. The pub name should be the focus both on the building itself and as depicted on the pictorial sign.

Avoid over-signing and keep the information boards to a minimum. Avoid meaningless phrases like 'chilled lagers' and 'wines and spirits' as every pub and inn sells these. The message must be good food, hospitality, service and friendliness. This can be achieved by a combination of signage, decor, hanging baskets and charm, not by a proliferation of signs telling you these things (Figure 4.2).

The effectiveness of advertising is always a difficult thing to measure. How much value do you get from a £100 advertisement in your local paper? How effective is a mail drop in target housing areas and nearby offices? Does a local radio series of advertisements help?

The answers to these questions have to be hedged with doubts and qualifications. Value for money in advertising is notoriously hard to pin down. Even the major companies with huge budgets for market research can get it wrong.

So tread warily when it comes to advertising, do not get talked into taking space in unsuitable or expensive publications. Keep your target market in your mind and aim at these – the 'scatter gun' approach is wasteful.

When you advertise, you must tell the reader or listener something which is interesting, which will claim his attention. Only advertise when you have something to say: a new menu, a new restaurant, a special Christmas lunch or the launch of a special guest ale policy.

Whether you are promoting your inn by advertisement, leaflet or letter, the image you present must be consistent and reflect the style and quality of your establishment. A quality-food operation can be damaged by being presented in an advertising feature of a local newspaper where all the other advertisers are offering downmarket, cheap and cheerful food.

However stylish your advertising, you will find it hard to know whether it is effective. Henry Ford is reputed to have said 'I know 50 per cent of my advertising is wasted, the trouble is, I don't know which 50 per cent'.

Your simplest way of attempting to evaluate the cost-effectiveness of your advertising is to discreetly ask new customers, whenever you get the opportunity, how they came to hear of your inn – and keep a record of the answers to check against the expenditure on advertising. There is a more direct way: to

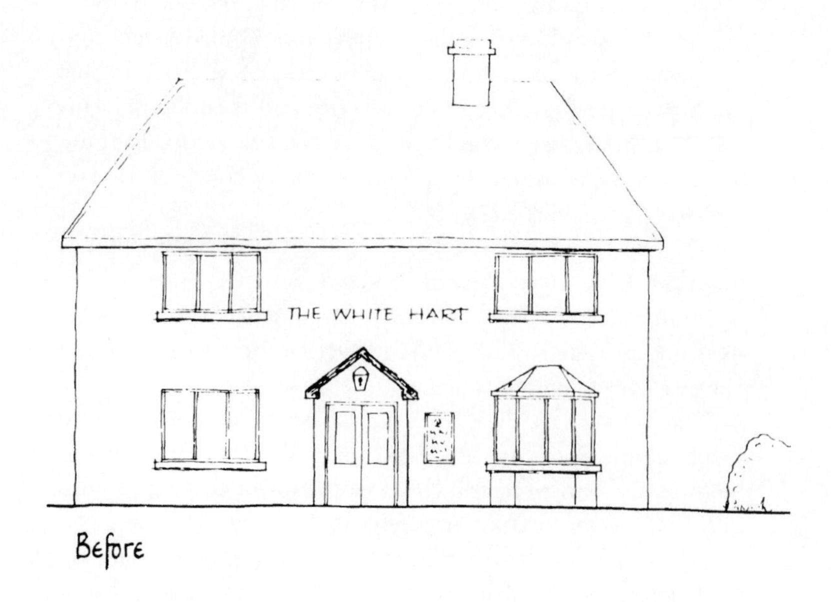

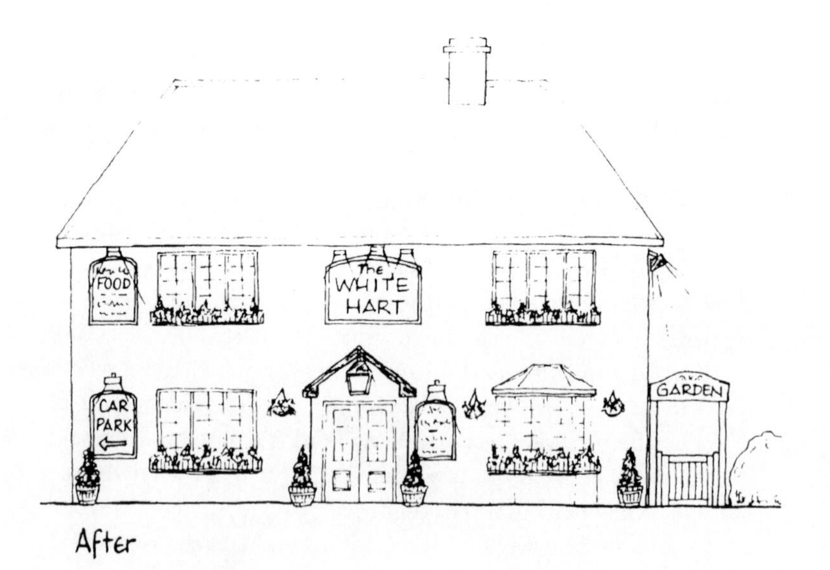

Figure 4.2 An example of how good signing, plants and lighting can improve the external appeal of a pub or inn

contain within your advertisement a coupon or special offer such as 'a free half-bottle of wine with a two-course dinner for two'. To qualify customers must bring the advertisement with them. This can work well and certainly helps to monitor the response. Remember not to leave the offer open-ended. Set a time limit or restriction of say 'only one coupon per couple' or, if you are already packed out on a Saturday evening, qualify it further 'valid Monday to Friday evenings'. But special offers and coupons need to be viewed carefully: does a special offer reflect the right image for your inn? Or could it smack of the cut-price supermarket?

This is where the importance of having a totally clear perception of what your inn projects and who your target customers are becomes vital.

One of the best advertisements is entry into one of the recognized pub guides. An entry in Egon Ronay or the Good Pub Guide is worth much more than any newspaper advertising campaign. Encourage your satisfied customers to write in to the guides' editors and recommend your inn. The reputable guides will only list you if your operation is a good one but they will not even know about you unless people write in and tell them.

There are several other guidebooks where you pay to enter. These may be useful but it is possible that you will see little benefit from them. As part of your decision, ask to see the existing pub guide and see who else is in there. You will find that often anyone prepared to pay the price, however poor their operation, will be included and it cannot be in your interest to be listed alongside them.

Local Tourist Boards can be a valuable source of reference for a traditional quality inn, particularly one that offers rooms to let.

Word-of-mouth is the most powerful advertisement of all. It can, of course, work both ways and can be very damaging if you are slow to get your act together. It takes time to build a reputation and, contrary to popular belief, it takes time to lose it again. A visit to a former Egon Ronay 'pub of the year' where the new owners had clearly lost their way bears testament to this. The operation was poor but they were still busy although, sadly from their point of view, not for very much longer.

The general local

When thinking of what is the true British pub, many of us will refer to a traditional inn but the general local pub is an even bigger segment of the licensed trade.

You will find these on the edges of large towns, in market towns and villages. They will often have had two bars but many will have been 'modernized' during the last twenty years and converted to one bar. They are, as you will have read, similar in some ways to the estate local but will draw their trade from a greater cross-section of people and from a much wider geographical spread.

Core custom

The general local will draw custom from nearby businesses, offices, salesmen and other men and women at lunchtime who will be attracted by the value-for-money food. Older locals may also visit at lunchtime.

Early evening is again dominated by workers on their way home and a few locals of mixed age. The core custom comes mainly from the B, C1 and C2 social groups at both lunchtime and evening.

Later in the evening, regulars will visit from as far afield as five miles, midweek mainly male and attracted by pub games such as pool and darts. The trade tends to be younger midweek but slightly older, thirty plus, at the weekends. At weekends, more couples use the pub and the games area gives way to the lounge bar.

The main purpose of the customer's visit

At lunchtime, the majority are there to eat good value food. In the evening and at weekends, the principal reason is to drink and meet friends. Games and teams are a major draw to this style of pub and some of the more successful ones will have a team event most weekday evenings. They may also sponsor soccer or other teams and these too will draw custom on training nights and match days.

Music is often featured at weekends, especially in larger pubs, and this is also one of the motivations for using the pub.

Service and style

Like all pubs and inns, continuity and reliability are essential ingredients for success. Service levels do not have to be slick and fast but friendly and caring. The atmosphere needs to be relaxed and the licensee and staff need to greet their customers like friends. It is a more personal business than a traditional inn, the customers are more regular and often consider the pub as 'their' pub. The organization of teams by the pub adds to this feeling of belonging. It is not possible to run a successful local in an impersonal way; the licensee must be involved and should be the catalyst that gets the social life of the pub going.

Midday food should be on offer to exploit fully the potential of the general local. Portions need to appear generous (even if it is just an extra large helping of chips) and, although not necessarily cheap, it must appear to offer full value.

Although food may be served in the evenings, it could in many cases confuse the focus of the operation which should be drinking, teams and meeting friends. If food is offered in the evening, it should be cleared away by eight thirty or you may lose more in wet trade than you are gaining from food. An occasional barbecue is the exception to this rule but these are difficult to organize with an unpredictable climate.

Beer quality is most important. How often have you heard 'I don't go to The George because the beer is awful'? Strangely, the actual brew does not appear to be important although there is usually a hard core of customers who only drink one brewer's wares and think all other brews are rubbish.

It is up to the licensee to get teams up and running. He may even find that it is in his interest to pay subscriptions into the various leagues for his own pub teams. With soccer teams, it is often good policy to pay for the strip and supply the match balls. Although you can be taken advantage of, it is still a good use of your marketing budget to spend it on customers who may use your pub seven days a week. Although they are slightly dubious legally, weekend meat and other raffles can help to offset some of these costs.

Free snacks on a Sunday lunchtime is another piece of small expenditure that could bring in rich rewards.

Music will be played for most of your opening hours. This will probably come from a juke box. Compact disc juke boxes now dominate this market and have the advantage of being quite profitable as well. It is essential, though, to have sufficient speakers to prevent blare.

Live music is an occasional option but, as we explain further in Chapter 5, a potentially expensive one. Local pubs did suffer severely during the recession of the late eighties and early nineties and do now need constant activity to keep them full and their business healthy.

Products

A typical general local derives over 80 per cent of its total turnover from drinks sales (known as wet sales). It figures therefore that getting the product mix right is important. Fortunately, this is not too difficult. You will need at least three lagers, a premium lager like Stella Artois, a standard lager such as Carling and one of the Australian or Canadian lagers, Castlemaine, Fosters or Labatts. Although cask-conditioned ale sales are only just holding their own, year on year, it is important to have at least two of them; a standard bitter such as Tetley or Greene King IPA and a premium bitter, maybe Bass or Wadworths 6X. You will be judged on the quality of your cask-conditioned ale so make sure that you do not stock too many and consequently get slow throughputs. We cover this in more detail in Chapter 8. A smooth flow ale, perhaps Kilkenny or Caffreys is essential, as is a draught stout such as Guinness, Murphys or Beamish. A keg cider, say Strongbow, completes the draught range.

A full range of bottled premium lagers, premium ciders, ice lagers and ales are needed, prominently displayed on the shelves of your backfitting or in your glass fronted cooler cabinets. Your best profit products should be in the most eye catching positions. You may also have a slight demand for bottled stout, Guinness and Mackeson and a bottle-conditioned ale such as White Shield Worthington; sales of these products have been less than buoyant in recent years and their futures are not too bright.

Soft drinks usually enjoy a surprisingly high throughput. You will need to have post mix on some of the principal products, notably cola, lemonade and orange juice. The post mix system gives the advantage of service through coolers and, although the profit levels may be a little less than from using, say, large bottles of lemonade, the quality and ease of service make up for this. Do try your draught soft drinks from time to time because, although the supplier sets the syrup to carbonated water ratio (called the brix), this can sometimes get out of balance. Too much syrup and the drink is over-sweet and damaging to your gross profit margins or too little and the drink will taste watery.

It is better to sell your 'mixers' such as tonics and dry ginger in baby bottles. The profit level is excellent and the drink looks better when the gin, ice and lemon are served in the glass with the tonic served separately in its bottle.

Wines and spirits are likely to account for up to 15 per cent of your total wet trade and so are important. The range does not have to be as comprehensive as in a traditional inn. It is wise to use nationally known spirit and fortified wine brands rather than the slightly cheaper non-proprietary ones. A choice of two vodkas, two or more whiskies and two gins plus Bacardi white rum, Canadian Club whisky, a three star cognac, an 80° proof dark rum and a short range of liqueurs including Southern Comfort. Single malt whisky has a speciality following and one bottle of up to six well-known brands will add interest to your backfitting and may bring you some high margin sales.

Sherries, ports and vermouths are not the sellers they once were but you must have good cream, medium and fino sherry, one ruby port and a range of Cinzano or Martini. Other products come and go such as bottled cocktails and spiced rum but few become part of the essential product range so do not get tempted to order more than a bottle or two.

One reasonable red wine by the glass plus a dry and medium white are all that are necessary. The white could be served through pumps on the counter or from a wine cabinet. You are unlikely to get many sales by the bottle but this could be encouraged by displaying a few bottles in a wine tub on the backfitting.

The food menu should be based on speed of service and value for money. To get any worthwhile lunchtime trade in a general local, a reasonable food operation is vital Assuming that you have efficient extraction from your kitchen, then chips must form part of your menu. With healthy eating now a byword in many homes, ham, egg and chips and sausage and chips are increasingly in demand on a pub's menu from those who are only too eager to escape from the rigours of low-cholesterol diets. Up to half-a-dozen non-chip dishes including a vegetarian dish plus a couple of daily specials should complete your menu.

Decor, lighting, furnishings and facilities

There should be two distinct areas in this style of pub. It may be that you have two bars but, if not, the creation of a games area and a more comfortable lounge area is necessary.

The **lounge** should be fully carpeted using a traditional style of pub carpet. Although green and blue carpets may look smart in a private living room, they rarely work well in a pub. Remember to bear in mind the extent of area to be covered when choosing your pattern. A large patterned carpet can make a small bar appear smaller and a small patterned carpet can look almost plain in a large area. Plain carpets are rarely used because they more readily show burns and stains.

Furnishings in the lounge area should be fully upholstered and comfortable. Because of their dual use, tables, chairs and stools should be the correct height for the customers' ease of eating. Some areas of fixed seating are usually desirable.

Wall coverings are more often wallpaper than the painted walls found in a traditional inn. Although we have never quite understood why some male customers have the habit of leaning with the sole of one foot against the wall, it is often worth considering some more durable covering for the lower part of walls, especially in an area where customers may wish to stand. Pillars and exposed corners often get shabby very quickly and this should be in your mind when planning your decor.

Bric-a-brac should have some significance for the pub and its customers. Some of the most popular pictures are of the '1950 darts club outing to Skegness' or 'Church Lane and the village pump 1910' variety. Local pubs are about local people and your pictures on the walls should reflect this. The interests of the innkeeper or the name of the pub itself may also be reflected in the bric-a-brac, which is fine as long as the theme does not become excessive.

Wall lighting is usually better than overhead and a good quality lighting scheme can do wonders for your pub.

The **games area** will have 'harder' finishes. A wood, stone or lino-covered floor rather than carpet; loose seating and tables suitable for cribbage, dominoes or esoteric local games such as euchre as well as an overflow for eaters at lunchtime.

If space permits, then a pool table will become a valuable amenity as well as a useful source of income. Profits of £100 a week or more can be made from a busy pool table. It is important that there is sufficient space for the pool table: a six by nine foot table in order to allow for adequate cueing space ideally needs an area of fifteen by eighteen feet, bigger than the average domestic sitting room. Cueing across walkways to the toilets or exits is a permanent source of irritation and can, on occasion, cause violence.

An excellent and possibly raised darts throw complete with spotlights, electronic and manual scoreboards will bring in useful custom. With women's as well as men's darts teams, trade may be generated on most weekday evenings by encouraging your customers to join your darts team.

Pool players are on average younger than darts players and to have both games in the same pub needs space. It is difficult to block off the darts throw for a pool match or vice versa and this too can cause unpleasantness. So, unless you have enough space, decide on one game or the other. A word of warning: pub teams, whatever the game or sport, can be a source of custom and profit but they can also cause you difficulties. They may become too demanding of your time, expect too much in the way of free drinks or free food at home matches or become over-dominant in the bar and upset your other regulars. Visiting teams can also be a problem; their behaviour may be such that you would not normally be prepared to accept it.

The lesson is that it is you who must run the pub as you want it for the good of the business as a whole; you cannot allow your teams to run you!

Quiz machines, which can pay out prizes of up to £10, known as SWPs (skill with prizes) and video machines known as AWOPs (amusement without prizes) often have an important role in a general local. These need to be well-sited and should never take space from the darts or pool areas. Take care not to over-cater for this market or you have your bar looking like a licensed amusement arcade.

The most important machines to site are the AWPs (amusement with prizes). In a good machine house, these could net you upwards of £5,000 and exceptionally as much as £20,000 a year. Siting is critical and the main pub-operating companies employ experts who will seek out the best location for the AWPs, sometimes doubling the income by moving them from one location in the pub to another. The machines themselves always need to be new and exciting and it therefore pays to rent rather than buy. We cover this subject more thoroughly in Chapter 7. Remember, though, that you need a permit from the Licensing Justices to operate an AWP on your premises and the number they allow is limited.

Juke boxes play an important part in the music needs of this style of pub. Compact disc juke boxes are now commonplace and, with their vast capacity, can cater for most music tastes. Again, it is vital to have sufficient speakers with individual volume control from behind the bar to allow you to have full control over noise levels and allow for quieter areas in the pub.

Good-quality toilets are required, with the Ladies having an even higher standard than the traditional inn. It is desirable that the Ladies should be easily accessible from the lounge bar without the need for customers to pass through the games area which sometimes can be intimidating.

Advertising and promotions

It is easy for an inexperienced licensee to be talked into buying space in a publication which is unsuitable or poor value for money. If an advertisement salesman calls on you or telephones to try to sell space, particularly in a publication unfamiliar to you, avoid instant decisions – give yourself the opportunity to think through the salesman's proposal. Is the publication genuine, when will it be published, what is the circulation, how many readers does it have, do the readers match your target customers in terms of age, social groups and geography, what will it cost you to reach each of those target customers by this medium and is there a better, more effective way?

Be as parsimonious as possible with your advertising budget until you are confident of the right medium which works for your pub – and you can prove it through increased turnover.

In our view, it is rare for a general local to get great benefit from a newspaper advertisement. As the name suggests, 'locals' are frequented by people living or working nearby. Word-of-mouth is the most usual way that a good or a bad local becomes known. A leaflet drop to local offices showing your menu will bring benefits and perhaps a mail drop through selected local front doors advertising a special pub event will give your trade a lift. Publicity is gained from your own noticeboards or posters advertising your teams, your football club, a quiz night or a party night. The latter are key activities for general local pubs and, done well, can generate a lot of extra business.

Support for the parish magazine or local events need not be expensive but is a wise move to confirm your role in the local community. Free publicity gained from the local newspapers or radio stations can enhance the standing of the general local: the media are often keen to pick up a story from a pub, particularly if it has a 'human interest' angle or concerns charity fundraising.

Summary

In this chapter, we have concentrated on two of our pub types – the traditional food-led inn and the general local. The principle of looking at each aspect of the business in detail to establish the most appropriate and profitable operation for a particular pub or inn applies to all pub types.

- Make your customer proposition clear, not only to your customers, but to yourself and your staff.
- Understand the customers you are targeting and set out your stall to meet their needs.
- Continuity and reliability of service, product and hospitality are the keys to success.

5 Running the business

The previous chapter has explained how you should present your business to the public, how you establish your image and how you project your inn or pub as the best place for your target customers to eat or drink.

In this chapter, we deal with the practical detail of the operation covering the physical aspects of the business and the equipment used.

Bar layout

The focal point of the pub is the bar, that is, the area from which drinks are dispensed and often referred to as the servery. Even in the food-led traditional inns, it is usually to the bar that customers turn first.

The bar is, in a sense, the bridge of the ship from which the action is controlled. Customers are normally first greeted by the innkeeper or his/her staff from behind the bar counter. It follows that the presentation of the bar and its siting are vital ingredients in the success and smooth running of the business.

When the customer comes through the door, he or she should immediately be aware of the bar's location or should be signposted to the area where the bar is to be found.

The bar itself should look attractive, interesting and cared for, but it also has to be practical for those working behind it. There are three elements to the bar: the counter, the backfitting and the working space between, and we will look at each of these in some detail (see Figure 5.1).

The counter

The best and most practical counters are of solid hardwood which takes plenty of polish and from which spillage is easily wiped. There are counters made of stone, copper and other natural materials but these all have disadvantages when compared with hardwood. Plastic counter tops, which happily are tending to be things of the past, have practical and aesthetic drawbacks.

The height of the counter is very important. It needs to be a convenient height for customers but also for staff dispensing drinks. This will enable staff to serve cask-conditioned ale through beer engines without too much back-bending. Many an aching back or a strained muscle can be avoided by good bar design.

Ergonomics only came into bar design in the 1980s and you find many bar counters less than ideal. Quite often, the counter is much too high and this makes it appear as a barrier to customers; in others the floor is raised behind the counter giving the customer a worm's eye view of the landlord's backside, not a pretty sight in some cases.

Of course, most innkeepers have to make do with the bar counter that is there. It is often impossible and always expensive to rebuild a bar counter to a different height or in a new location.

Think carefully about the positioning of the beer, cider and soft drink dispense points on your bar, particularly the tall draught ale handpulls. They must give a coherent message to your customers but also be placed to the best advantage for you and your staff with the most used taps easiest to reach. In busier pubs where you could expect to take £800 or more in one session, then you must consider 'doubling up' and creating separate work stations. Figure 5.2 shows how this operates with the lesser selling brands between the two work stations. Naturally, in very busy pubs with many bar staff, you may need more separate work stations.

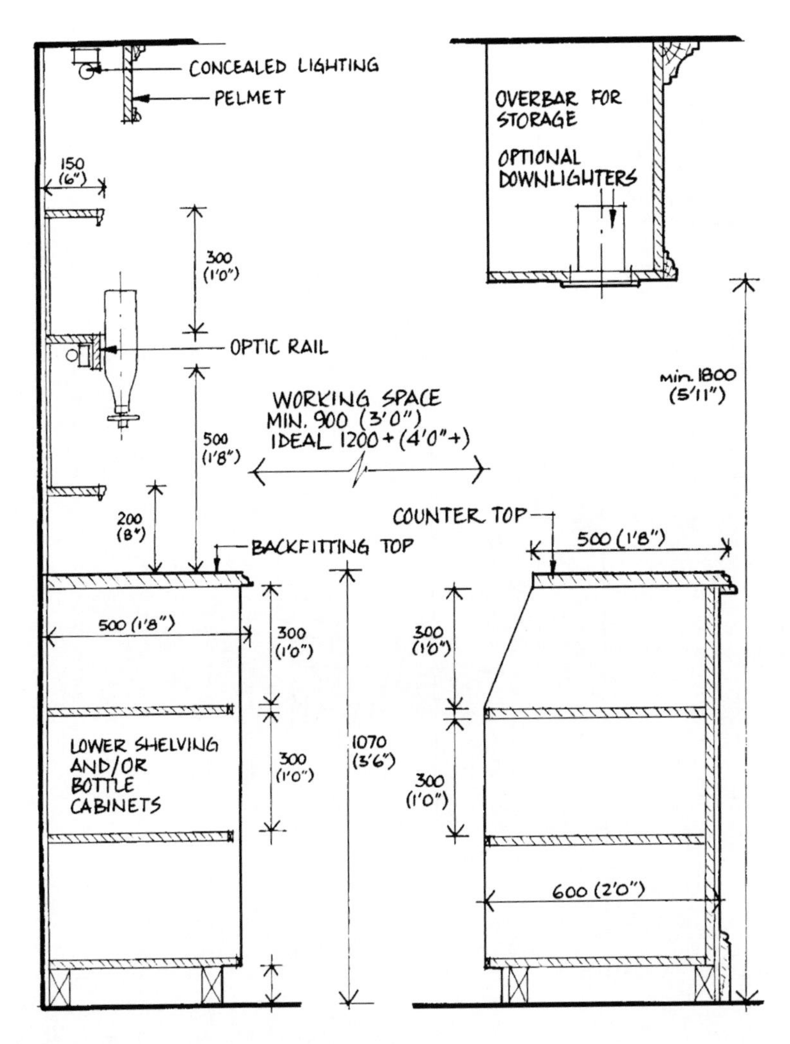

Figure 5.1 Design for a bar counter, backfitting and working space

The introduction of new products, greatly increased in recent years, and the changes in public taste and local preferences mean that you have to be constantly aware of what your customers will enjoy and tailor your bar accordingly. Figure 5.2 can only be one representation of a product range.

However, be wary of having under-used or superfluous taps. Every pipe you have connecting cellar with dispense point will

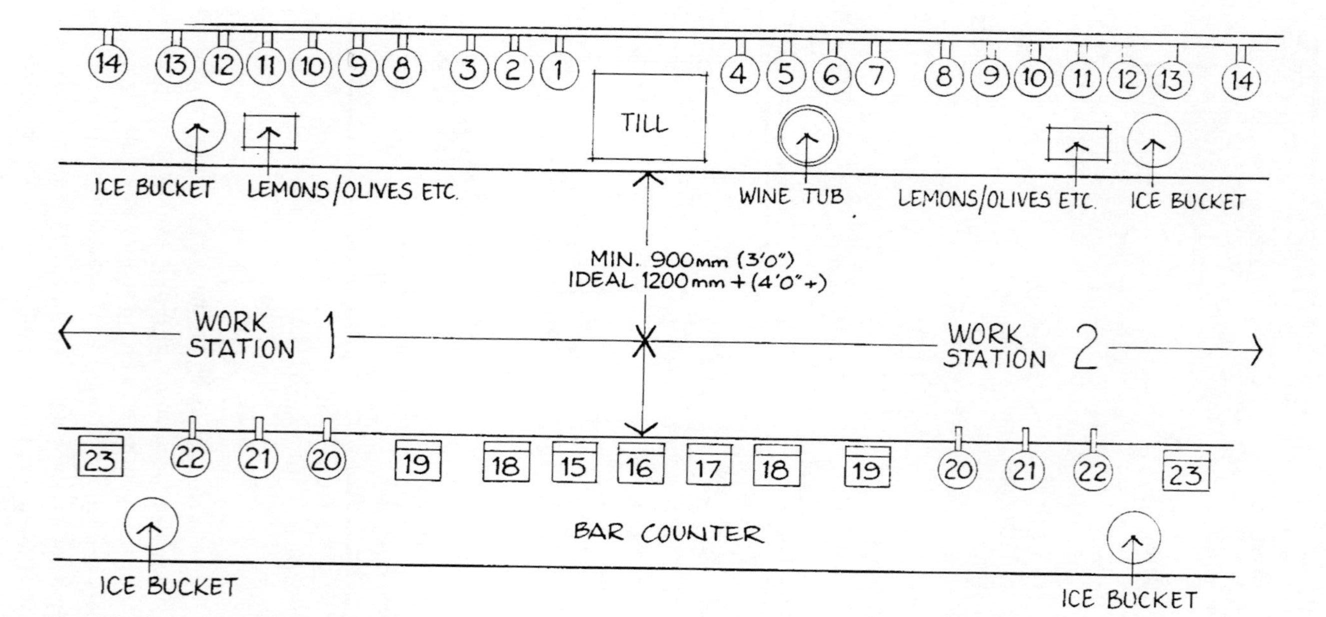

Figure 5.2 Work stations for a moderately busy bar. *Key:* 1, malt whisky; 2, cognac; 3 dark rum; 4. Pernod/Ricard; 5, vermouth; 6, vermouth; 7, vermouth; 8, vodka; 9, whisky; 10, gin; 11, white rum; 12, second whisky; 13, second gin; 14, other slower moving products; 15, cider; 16, stout; 17, smooth flow bitter; 18, standard plus lager; 19, standard lager; 20, beer engine/cask ale; 21, beer engine/cask ale; 22, beer engine/cask ale; 23 premium lager.

be full of expensive liquor which, if not sold quickly, will have to be thrown away and every pipe has to be cleaned each week with some inevitable wastage.

The bar counter needs to be a practical width for your serving needs and to have the necessary storage space beneath it. Most glassware is stored under the counter rather than on the backfitting so the shelf surfaces need to be fully cleansable to comply with environmental health needs.

Finally, the bar flap which allows you to get into and out of the bar should be positioned for minimum disruption to customers and to the work space behind the bar.

The backfitting

This is the licensee's prime showcase for his drinks range. It should be appropriate to the style of the operation. You would not, for instance, have a prominent display of 'Taboo' in a traditional inn or a range of fine old cognacs in a young persons' pub. The backfittings and the products displayed should be sparklingly clean, uncluttered and of course laid out in a way that will be convenient and efficient for staff to use. The display should focus customers' attention on the items the innkeeper is most keen to sell: perhaps his wide choice of malt whiskies; the special selection of Australian white wines; the large range of imported premium bottled lagers.

Much thought should be given to the positioning of the most commonly ordered drinks. For instance, if gin and tonic is a major seller, make sure the gin bottle or bottles on optic are in the best place relative to the tonic bottles and that the lemon and ice are also as conveniently placed as possible. Your aim in bar layout is to make the service of drinks quick and efficient as well as to make it a showcase. It may also be appropriate to promote the food available with, say, a chalkboard for the bar showing today's specials.

Whatever the backfitting does, it should help you to sell and enhance your reputation as a quality, professional innkeeper. Nothing does more damage to your image than a dirty, ill-lit, cluttered, scruffy backfitting.

Some obvious things to avoid:

- prime selling space taken up with rows of glasses;
- a jumble of out-of-date notices, showcards, posters etc.;
- invoices and letters stuffed down by the side of the till;
- empty bottles on optics;
- unpolished bottles and dusty decorative glassware;
- unpolished mirrors on the backfitting;
- grubby-looking displays of nuts and snacks on cards.

Sadly, the list could go on – it is only too easy to bring to mind the many ways in which the unprofessional innkeeper allows his selling space to be wasted and lets himself down with an appalling backfitting. If you extend the selling space to the bar counter, there is nothing like dirty ashtrays, wet drip towels and pools of beer to put off a potential customer before he has even ordered.

One of the golden rules for pubs and inns is:

- be clean, be tidy and be organized.

The increasing demand for cold or cooled drinks, which has been general in the trade for over twenty years, has only slowly been satisfied. In particular, bottled lagers, white wines and soft drinks need to be cooled to meet customer demand. The old-style open cold shelf has always been a poor and inefficient way to cool a product; the cabinets with glass doors are much to be preferred and have the additional advantage of prominently displaying the products as well.

Up to a few years ago, wines were commonly dispensed through optics from wall-mounted cooled cabinets. These are, however, less than perfect both functionally and aesthetically.

The measure appeared to be mean (although it was not) and, because they were bulky, the cabinets were usually tucked away in a 'dead' area of the backfitting.

One of the best ways of marketing and selling white wine in traditional inns is by use of a wooden ice tub on the backfitting or counter. There are successful innkeepers, some of them pioneers in the huge growth of wine sales, who use this method. If it is managed well and turnover is speedy, it can be a most pleasing and effective way of promoting sales, not only of wine by the glass but by the bottle as well. If, in addition to this, you keep your back-up stock in a glass-fronted cabinet built into the backfitting, you will have the best of ancient and modern, although at a price, because the cabinets are expensive.

There are various devices available which allow you to seal a bottle and keep the contents fresh during slack periods or overnight. Wine is now important in so many pubs that it is well worth every effort to not only provide good quality wine to start with but to maintain that quality throughout the life of the bottle.

In locals and young persons' pubs, where sales warrant it, draught dispense may be the answer. The wine is kept in three-litre or ten-litre packs in the cellar and then dispensed through miniature and sometimes rather twee 'wine pulls' on the counter. This method tends to upset the purists and it certainly takes the mystique out of wine-drinking which is why it is not recommended for traditional inns. It does, however, deliver a consistent product at the right temperature with the quality as good as the innkeeper is able or prepared to buy.

The working space

The space between the backfitting and the bar counter is the stage on which you and your staff perform. It will, at times, be extremely busy and overcrowded. Your job is to make this working space as agreeable as possible (see Figure 5.1).

The ideal depth between bar counter and backfitting allows staff room to operate efficiently, moving between the bar and the backfitting with the minimum of wasted effort. You must plan the positioning of the key elements to avoid confusion and interference.

These key elements could include, for instance, the till or tills, the section of the bar counter most favoured by customers when ordering, the draught beer engines, the gin or whisky optics, the ice buckets or the intercom for putting food orders through to the kitchen.

Insofar as you are able, ensure that these elements are positioned so that you and your staff can operate to your best advantage without continually having to push past each other or to wait unnecessarily to use an optic or the till. Very often, it will only be by trial and error and experience that the best layout will be achieved.

You can make things easier for yourself by avoiding the more obvious pitfalls and these are a few basic rules to bear in mind:

- avoid pinch points;
- store beer glasses near the service points;
- allow space on the counter without beer taps through which to serve;
- remember glass-washing is a space-consuming operation;
- avoid customer blindspots to ensure that, even if he or she cannot see you, you can certainly see him/her.

We can all remember pubs where the till is exactly opposite the beer engines and the landlord's backside sticking out as he is pulling a pint with the landlady jammed between him and the till drawer. The strange thing is they may well have been working like that for years but luckily they have never been busy! We have also seen short bar staff stretching to serve drinks over the lager fonts and spilling more than they serve. These problems are usually unnecessary with just a little planning.

Lighting in the bar and backfitting is important. It must be efficient and practical to give sufficient light for staff to see clearly particularly around the till and other key work places; it should show off your important products to best advantage; it should create an impression of activity and professionalism. But it must also be sympathetic to the atmosphere of the whole establishment; it must not be over-bright and dazzle the customers; it is working at its best when customers are not even aware of the attention you have paid to it. The most effective lighting is nearly always achieved when there is a mix of sources, differing light values and variations of colour and style in light fittings. Fluorescent strip lights as a main light source are guaranteed to kill the atmosphere in a bar servery – avoid them at all costs!

For all aspects of operating the bar, you need always to have in mind that it is a food-handling area (drinks are food as far as the health and hygiene legislation is concerned). This subject is dealt with in Chapter 8 but you must expect that the Environmental Health Officer (EHO) will demand that in your bar servery all work surfaces, shelves and floors are of sound impervious material that is readily cleanable; that there are appropriate glass-washing facilities and a separate hand-washing basin complete with soap and towel in or near the servery.

Glasses

The style and quality of glasses you offer your customer says much about your inn or pub. Badly designed or inappropriate glasses are irritating to customers and can even lose a repeat sale. This can apply at either end of the social spectrum; in many parts of the country the public bar customer will insist on a 'straight glass' for his pint and will look with disdain on a dimpled mug; in the lounge bar a customer will feel less than happy with a glass of wine served in a small, mean, thick or ugly glass.

A surprisingly high number of customers feel strongly about receiving their drink in the appropriate glass. It costs very little more, in the context of your overall business, to get the correct glass for each type of drink and you will find your customers really appreciate it.

There are excellent ranges of glasses available from manufacturers and trade suppliers. Look at them all and choose carefully because you will need to take in to account durability and price as well as style and appearance.

But be careful – many alcoholic drinks have to be sold in measures defined by law (see Chapter 11). Do not get caught out with large stocks of glasses that will be made obsolete by new legislation.

Glass-washing

The EHOs, with good reason, have strong views on glass-washing facilities in the licensed trade. They will insist on an ample supply of hot water, appropriate detergent and hygienic drying arrangements.

These rules can be adequately met by a good-sized stainless steel sink and drainers and plentiful clean drying-up cloths. The glass-washing sink cannot be used for any purpose other than glass-washing because of the risk of cross-infection.

Increasingly, the busy pub or inn is moving to glass-washing cabinet machines either in the bar servery or ideally in a separate area off the bar dedicated to this purpose. There is a large range of this type of glass-washer available. Identify your needs, paying particular attention to size and space available and output. Perhaps check the machine in a recently refurbished managed house. The buyers in these big operations keep right up-to-date with the latest technology so it can be useful to indirectly pick their brains. Remember, it's not just the machine that takes up space but the racks for glasses too. Consider the plumbing needs, the after-sales service and the cost of installation when making your decision.

An establishment using a glass-washer is likely to need a bigger stock of glasses than one in which the glasses are hand-washed in smaller batches. However, an efficient glass-washing machine should save on staff costs.

A rather unpleasant thought for the average drinker is that, in a few pubs and inns, the machine is not cleaned internally from one month to the next and a quick look inside at the green slime would certainly put them off their drinks. Glass-washers need regular cleaning just like all equipment used in the bar, cellar or kitchen.

Ice-making machines

All pubs and inns nowadays need a reliable supply of ice; the market is well catered for with ice-making machines at varying prices and capacities. Weigh up your needs using similar criteria to those outlined for glass-washers. It is better to have too much ice than not enough and, like most machines, they usually last longer when purring along at half-capacity. Base your calculations on the busiest, hottest week of the year and you should then get one of sufficient size.

The innkeeper's prayer for all equipment servicing the bar or kitchen is:

'Do not break down'

He or she then usually adds with fingers crossed:

'Especially at a Bank Holiday weekend'.

One golfing innkeeper who did trust in prayer had a nasty habit of hitting his golf ball into the lake at the fifth. On asking God's help, he was told 'Keep your head down and swing slowly and all will be well'. The golfer said 'Thank you, God' and put down a new ball on the tee only for God to shout 'Not a new ball, you fool'.

However, because the professional innkeeper does not trust to luck or even prayer, he or she makes sure that there is a 100 per cent reliable emergency call-out service available for those key items of equipment without which the operation cannot function fully.

An ice-maker uses electricity to lower the temperature and create the ice. It also creates excess heat which has to be expelled so try to find a site where this does not create a problem.

Tills

The last fifteen years have seen dramatic changes in the way in which money transactions have been handled in pubs and inns. Once there was the cash drawer or the manual till, now there is available an array of the most sophisticated equipment including electronic point-of-sale (EPOS) to even rival those of supermarkets.

The modern tills can offer a range of facilities; keeping a running stock level, recording sales volumes of individual products or product groups, sales by individual bar or restaurant staff, gross profit percentages, analysis of sales by hour or session and many more. Tills may also be linked to a monitor in, for instance, the innkeeper's office. These systems provide a wealth of information for management; learning to use them effectively is the skill that needs to be gained. Equipment like this does not come cheap, you have to make it work for you to get full value from it.

When planning the layout of a backfitting, the type of till must be known. If you are using EPOS, the wiring required is considerable. Will the tills be built into the bar counter or free-standing on the backfitting? Will the till drawer be fixed to the till or sited separately? If the till selected has a price display pod on the top, will it fit under the optics? You only have to look at some pubs in your own locality to find how often the till has been sited as an afterthought.

Staff and prices

You must be concerned that your staff charge customers the correct price for their food or drink. With EPOS or preset tills, this should be guaranteed. It is your responsibility to see that prices are clearly marked on the beer taps, optics and shelves and that there is a priced list of lesser-used products readily available for staff to check whilst they are working. This particularly applies to products that may change from day to day or week to week – 'dishes of the day' or 'guest ale of the week' for example.

See Chapter 11 for the law on prices and price lists.

Furniture

Furniture in a bar or restaurant must look right but it must also be practical.

Tables must be 'readily cleansable' in the EHOs' favourite phrase. This means bar tables must repel drink stains and take a hot lunch plate without flinching. Hardwood table tops and good polish are the answers. Restaurant tables, if cloths and mats are used, may have less demanding requirements. It is essential that all tables and chairs be of suitable height for the purpose intended. If you are planning to develop even the most modest food trade, the low tables, favoured in the 1970s but still often in use, are totally unsuitable. Nothing is more uncomfortable than crouching over a table, under which your knees do not fit, trying to eat your bar meal.

A mix of size and shape of table creates the best ambience but a rectangular table is ideal for dining areas. It accommodates people more easily and can be pushed up to its neighbour to create a larger unit as required in a way that round tables cannot.

So a mix of shapes for ambience but a bias towards rectangular for operational reasons. Similarly, the diners' comfort is improved if tables are reasonably spaced – apart from anything else the customer is offered greater privacy and your staff can move between the tables more easily. Dining chairs in particular must be comfortable but sturdy.

Stools are useful in a bar; high ones for sitting at the bar and low ones for fitting in where space would not allow a chair. Great care must be taken in deciding the number of bar stools you will have. Too many and other customers are greeted by a sea of backs and hardly a sight of the bar counter. One per four foot run of bar is about the sensible maximum.

Bench seats, whether a modern 'banquette' or a re-utilized church pew, have their uses but have the disadvantage of being inflexible in a way that chairs are not.

Floor coverings

Many of the more sophisticated bar restaurants have areas that do not have carpet but rely upon the character of natural materials: York stone, tiles, old boards and sometimes a mixture. Ironically, this is a reversion to many an old-style pub floor before fitted carpets were thought of.

Linoleum, the non-slip variety, is a practical answer in certain high traffic areas like bar serveries or kitchens; loose rugs are used to effect on natural surfaces – provided that they are not a hazard to customers; carpet remains the most popular floor covering for most bars and restaurants. In drinks-led traditional inns, too much fitted carpet should be avoided, if possible.

Carpets for the licensed trade have to be:

- extremely hard-wearing,
- resistant to burns,
- of a type not to show stains readily,
- easy to clean regularly without doing damage.

As you will guess, a carpet of this type is expensive but you cannot afford to lower your specification.

The classic carpet therefore is a high quality grade five (80 per cent wool and 20 per cent nylon) Axminster or Wilton in a patterned design. Such a carpet could be expected to have a life of five or more years in an averagely busy area but we have known best-quality carpets to have needed replacement within eighteen months in exceptionally high traffic areas. The greatest area of wear on a pub or inn carpet is in front of the entrance from the kitchen and the counter flap but also the area around the bar counter. This is why you often see a metre-wide strip of linoleum in front of the bar counter with fitted carpet elsewhere in the room. It is effective but often spoils the look of the room. Regular cleaning is one of the answers to getting extra life from pub carpets.

Fire precautions

Although we tackle this subject in its legal sense in Chapter 11, no chapter covering the practical side of furnishings can be written without some reference to fire precautions.

The use of fire-resistant materials is now compulsory when refurbishing a bar or restaurant or indeed letting bedrooms. When taking over a business, check whether the furnishings are fire-resistant. Take advice from your local fire service and follow their advice to the letter. Fires in pubs or inns occur too regularly for the subject to be treated lightly. Take care when buying upholstered seats and fixed seating that they do not contain any foam plastic that gives off toxic fumes in case of fire.

Beware of plastic ceiling tiles which are often deadly when exposed to the heat of a fire.

Buy purpose-made ash buckets for emptying ashtrays into and never empty the contents into a non-metal bin.

Heating

One of the innkeeper's highest items of expenditure is on heat, light and power. Whatever the fuel source, it is likely to rank after staff costs as the biggest item of controllable expenditure. Energy conservation is therefore an important consideration and we deal with this more fully in Chapter 7. But how you heat your bars or dining area is important to you and your customers.

You need heating to be as economical as possible but consistent with customer comfort and ambience created. The customers' comfort is all-important; if they are enjoying your hospitality in an agreeable temperature, neither too hot in summer nor too cold in winter, the likelihood is they will stay on for another drink or a second course and be more likely to visit you again.

The old conundrum comes to mind; is an inn cold because it is empty or empty because it is cold? We, like you, have shivered in too many cold pubs to be in much doubt about the answer.

Your heating needs to be flexible, readily controlled by you or your staff to take account of changing conditions. The room that needs its heating on full at 7 pm may need no heating at all by 9.30 when it is packed. Ideally, you need a central heating system that is controlled by zonal thermostats but with the additional benefit of visual coal or gas fire.

Full air-conditioning is currently rare in Britain's pubs and inns but there is clear evidence that it is growing in popularity and can help the trade in an exceptionally busy operation especially on a hot summer's evening. Many cinemas, clubs and supermarkets are now air-conditioned and, although it is expensive to install and to run, it could well be money well-spent in the right circumstances.

For the great majority of licensed premises in Britain, the scene is very different with a wide mixture of heat sources, some, it has to be said, highly inefficient. In the traditional inn, an open fire of coal and logs does much to create that elusive quality, atmosphere; so much sought-after, so rarely found. An open fire looks welcoming and the faint smell of wood smoke is a marvellous bonus. It has the disadvantage of not being quickly damped down if the room gets too hot and it certainly needs man hours, or perhaps more often woman hours, to keep it cleaned out and always at its best. An open fire creates dust and extra room cleaning but we agree with the many innkeepers who believe that all the inconveniences are worthwhile for the extra consumer benefits that a real fire offers.

It is important to use your fireplace creatively in summer or when the fire is not lit. An empty grate is an unlovely sight. Fill it with flowers, plants, piles of logs or anything attractive and in keeping. A fireplace is a natural focus: make the most of it.

Smoke extraction and extractor fans

Extractor fans have been a feature of pubs for many years. When most people smoked, the tolerance to a smoky atmosphere was much greater and these extractor fans seemed efficient enough. They are expensive to run as they extract the air that has cost you so much to heat but, even so, do not really do a good job on cigarette smoke, especially in a low ceilinged inn. Fewer people are smoking and non-smokers (and particularly ex-smokers) are becoming intolerant of other people's smoke. An investment in an air purifier, of sufficient size to do the job, is an alternative, especially in a traditional inn. These can be leased, rented or purchased.

Music

PRS, PPL and VPL

Music is a vexed subject which the innkeeper needs to consider carefully. All forms of music played in a public room will cost money in the guise of an annual licence fee to PRS (Performing Rights Society). If a juke box, a video juke box or a taped music system is hired, the owner of the equipment will pay a fee to PPL (Phonographic Performance Ltd) or VPL (Video Performance Ltd) and that fee will be reflected in the rent the innkeeper pays for the equipment.

You need to have a PRS licence before you play any music in your pub or inn whether radio, tapes, compact discs or live. You could be heavily surcharged if you operate without a licence. If you are operating the type of pub where discos are an occasional feature, you will also need to negotiate a fee with PPL. They have wide-ranging powers and you can be fined heavily and banned from playing recorded music if you ignore them.

PRS, PPL and VPL are all very helpful when approached correctly. They can make an innkeeper's life very difficult if their powers are under-estimated.

Live music

If you choose to have live music in your bar, you are limited to one or two performers in total during one opening pub session. If you plan to exceed this number or to invite customers to sing with the paid performers, you are obliged to apply for an Entertainment Licence from your local authority (see Chapter 11).

Juke boxes

The juke box and its more recent offspring, the video juke box, can be important and valuable aids in attracting business to a public bar or young persons' bar. They are not usually very profitable in themselves as the equipment is expensive and the hire charge or profit-sharing arrangements with the owners does not leave much change for the licensee. In a busy local pub, you could expect to get £50 to £75 per week. They can be a contributing factor in creating the atmosphere needed for targeting a certain market sector. They should have several speakers, each with its own volume control and with the licensee in charge of the volume control switch. It is probably not worth purchasing your own equipment as it will be costly to buy and invariably the music choice that you will have to supply will not be great enough to keep the juke box in constant use.

A profit-share arrangement is initially best whilst you test out profitability and, if you then find it is doing well, convert to straight rental.

Background music

Used in pubs and inns of all types for creating atmosphere and allowing customers to talk without feeling they are being overheard. As with juke boxes, it is vital that there are sufficient speakers and that the innkeeper has control of the choice of music and volume, adjusting each to suit the time of day, type and number of customers. Many licensees have no thought for these controls (they no longer hear the music themselves) and the 'background' degenerates into a noisy, ill-chosen sound which irritates and sometimes repels the customer. As stated in Chapter 4, music choice and quality is vital so do not delegate it to your staff.

The real cost of music

Any music provided in a pub or inn, whether recorded or live, folk, rock, classical or jazz will not suit some of your customers: they will either dislike that particular type of music or the performer or both and will stay away.

Whether you are paying £20 for a semi-professional musician or £200 for a band, it is a financial outlay that should be measured carefully and in a number of ways.

To make paying for music worthwhile, you must attract extra customers. You must also make enough additional profit to justify not only the music costs but other direct costs as well such as advertising and additional staff. If, by having music on one night, you find that the trade on other nights of the week picks up as well because of the pub's slightly higher public profile, then this should be taken into your reckoning. Otherwise do the simple calculations shown in Figure 5.3.

	Without music	With music
	£	£
Evening takings	400	600
Gross profit 50%	200	300
Cost of music	Nil	100
Advertising music	Nil	20
Extra staff	Nil	20
Gross profit before other costs	200	160

Figure 5.3 The real cost of music

	Without music	With music
	£	£
Evening takings	400	700
Gross profit 50%	200	350
Cost of music	Nil	100
Advertising music	Nil	20
Extra staff	Nil	20
Gross profit before other costs	200	210

Figure 5.4 A near break-even calculation on music

You can see at a glance that, in spite of taking an extra £200, you have actually made less money. However, you might think it was just (but only just) worthwhile if the sums looked like those in Figure 5.4

Remember to think in gross profit and not in takings when absorbing additional costs like music.

Music in pubs or inns is important but remember:

- it can cost you as well as make you money;
- it can repel as well as attract custom;

- it must be controlled by the licensee;
- it must be appropriate to the customers you are trying to attract;
- it can detract as well as add to atmosphere;
- silence can sometimes be golden.

Pub gardens

There are five types of pub garden:

- those to look at;
- those to sit, eat and drink in;
- those designed for children to play in;
- a combination of the other three;
- vegetable gardens.

Each can earn the innkeeper money but each can cost money as well.

When assessing your perfect inn with its beautiful garden, try to remember how expensive it will be to maintain both in time and money. But do not let this put you off because, when the sun shines (which it sometimes does), customers always seek out the good pub gardens.

Decorative gardens

A beautiful well-kept garden, flower beds, tubs overflowing with blooms, window boxes or a mass of hanging baskets can create a wonderful effect and dress up the plainest building in a way that nothing else can.

Such pubs and inns are immediately attractive to customers because of the beauty of the display and because it shows from the outside that somebody cares. It is a statement about the innkeeper that is instantly recognizable whether from across the town square or in a country lane.

Most importantly, a flower or plant display can often be seen from a distance by a car driver or passenger; there is time to make a decision about stopping before slipping past the car park entrance. With luck, the car will have time to turn in and those dreaded words will not be heard: 'Oh well, we'll stop at the next pub'.

As was shown in Figure 4.2, it is astonishing what visual improvements can be made by skilled planting and tending but good gardening does not come cheap. If you are not a devoted gardener yourself or, more likely, will not have the time, then your enhancement of the pub is a cost factor you must take seriously. Assuming you have to buy most of your plants, fertilizers, containers and tools, you may well have a bill for several hundreds of pounds. Add to that the cost of labour and you could quite easily spend well over £1,000. If you know little about the subject and, especially if you are intending employing gardeners, then take advice. You should aim for:

- plants that give lots of show;
- plants with a long flowering life;
- plants needing little maintenance;
- perennials rather than annuals;
- planting schemes that use shrubs and trees to give colour and form to fill important spaces and ones that will grow and mature and improve with age;
- some area of hard surfaces such as paving, flagstones, free standing tubs and walls for variety.

Avoid anything that is:

- too time-consuming;
- too intricate and fiddly;
- poor value for money;
- labour-intensive.

Although window boxes and hanging baskets look terrific remember that they need watering up to twice each day in hot weather and will not really flourish unless they get regular feeding.

If you cannot keep them well, do not keep them at all.

Trade gardens

These include areas of lawn, patio and terrace which you wish to use as an extension of your inn's eating or drinking area during good weather. These should be:

- safe, i.e. separated from cars and free of other hazards;
- comfortable to eat and drink in;
- always kept clean and tidy and free from litter;
- easily maintainable which suggests simplicity;
- free of anything easily knocked over, broken or stolen;
- not too distant for service from the inn itself.

The benefits of a trade garden are:

- additional trading space during fine weather;
- an alternative drinking and eating environment for your customers, many of whom (when the weather is pleasant) will only visit pubs and inns that offer this facility;
- it attracts families with children who may not be allowed into the licensed premises itself because of the current licensing laws.

The disadvantages of trade gardens are:

- the comparatively high cost of setting up and maintaining;
- the relatively low usage because of dependence on our weather;
- staff costs for serving and clearing and difficulties of staff planning when the weather is unpredictable;
- the 'negative factor', especially in food-led traditional inns, where large numbers of occasionally unruly children may upset your core middle-aged market.

Always balance the effort and expenditure against the potential additional income but also remember that a pub or an inn without outside drinking facilities often trades at a lower than usual level when the weather is warm and sunny and therefore most successful innkeepers think the costs and inconveniences well worthwhile.

Children's play area

This may be part of, or in addition to, a trade garden and the same basic rules apply, although particular attention must be given to safety in all its aspects. It will include play equipment, whether simple swings and a climbing frame or more ambitious and costly adventure play equipment. In each case, it is the innkeeper's responsibility to see that the equipment is well-constructed and maintained and meets proper safety standards. The safety regulations are becoming increasingly onerous and it would be prudent to speak to your local authority's health and safety department before investing in new or assuming responsibility for existing equipment.

You should not buy domestic-quality play equipment as it will not be durable enough. Children's play equipment can cost from a modest £200 to well over £30,000 for a fully-fledged system. You may need planning permission for some of the more elaborate pieces like giant boots, especially if you are in a conservation area.

If children are not a key element in your marketing plan, then take care not to over-invest in play equipment.

Vegetable gardens

Not too many pubs and inns have vegetable gardens because they take up space that can usually be better used and they are heavy on labour. If it is the innkeeper's hobby, then there is some commercial benefit in home-grown vegetables but otherwise the cost of cultivation may make the vegetables produced too expensive.

A pleasant compromise is a herb garden which can look decorative and also give a competitive edge to the menu. The work involved is not heavy and will attract interest from customers, especially if the herbs are clearly labelled.

Car parks

Car parking has become an essential element in the success of most inns and many pubs. There are pubs in urban areas which draw their trade from nearby office workers, shoppers or others who have reason to be in the town but there are relatively few which earn their living from 'locals' who walk to the pub. This is in complete contrast to the 1950s when many inns and pubs generated almost all their trade from those living within walking distance.

The revolution in transport and the huge and continuing growth in car ownership and usage across all age groups, gender and class have transformed the pattern of trade across the country. The car brings into reach inns in villages and other rural locations that were only known to the local population during the first half of the twentieth century.

Today, the pub or inn may not be able to exist without a suitable car park or nearby parking. What should car parks offer?

- Strong, clear directional signs so that the driver sees the entrance clearly;
- safe entry from and exit to the road;
- a sound surface without potholes and puddles;
- encouragement for drivers to park neatly;
- good lighting to the car park and the paths from it;
- clear signing to the bar entrance from the car park;
- safety for pedestrians, especially children;
- cleanliness and tidiness at all times.

As with a pub garden, your car park says much about you and your standards. An untidy car park with thistles growing around the edges may actually lose you custom and will certainly give a negative message to customers.

However well kept, some car parks can be unattractive simply because they present a forbidding sea of black tarmac against which the pub sits uncomfortably. Resurfacing is expensive but it can often pay to soften the scene by creating a strip of grass or planting alongside the pub or with some heavy potted shrubs. You might decide to plant some shrubs around the perimeter of the car park or organize some more sympathetic lighting. But remember that, as with gardens, the shrubs should be practical, easy to maintain and be positioned in such a way that even the most errant car driver (of which you will undoubtedly have some) cannot damage them too severely. Kerbs need to be high enough, if possible, to stop cars damaging your plants and shrubs but not too high that your customers' cars are damaged.

It is your responsibility to see that the car park is a safe place for your customers; having ensured that, make sure you have a neat, clear sign stating that you cannot be held responsible for loss of, or damage to, cars parked there (also see Chapter 11).

If your rural inn is large, the car park small and there is no other local car parking, then the number of customers that you will attract will be dictated by the small car park not, sadly, by the large, half empty pub.

6 Staff and customers

If the most important people in your pub or inn are your customers, then the next most important are your staff. The men and women that you employ have to fit into the pattern that you have established as the most effective for your particular establishment. They should be capable of reflecting your style, whether out front or behind the scenes. They should have a talent and an aptitude for the business.

Selection of staff

All employers have different standards by which potential staff are judged but there are some qualities which may be considered fundamental:

- ability to relate to customers and other staff;
- a cheerful disposition and a ready smile;
- physical and mental dexterity;
- honesty;
- flexibility;
- reliability with a good health record;
- a willingness to learn;
- an understanding of the demands of the job.

You will notice that 'experience' is not included in this list. Many innkeepers are happier to take on staff who have the fundamental qualities and train them into the job. This way the staff learn only the good habits or at least the innkeeper's own bad habits, not anyone else's!

The qualities listed have largely to be assessed at the interview with the prospective employee although there is useful checking and follow-up work that can also be done.

Advertising for staff

This can be done in several ways:

- advertising in your local paper;
- a notice in a local shop window;
- by using your local job centre;
- by a notice inside or outside your premises;
- by word of mouth.

Only the first two cost you anything but do not be afraid of spending a few pounds to try and ensure that you attract the right applicants.

When advertising, make sure that your message is simple and crisp. Try to emphasize one or two of the main qualities you are seeking and do not try to give all the information in one small advertisement. The object of an advertisement is to get people to contact you. Although it takes valuable time, the more calls you receive the more chance you will have of getting the right applicant. Use the telephone to 'screen out' those that are clearly unsuitable. Prepare and have by the phone a short series of supplementary questions for this purpose such as hours and days, car driver, current job, experience, age, current or other employer. Remember that you are not allowed by law to discriminate by sex, race or colour and can get into problems with age too. You cannot use words like 'barmaid', 'waiter', 'young woman', 'white' or 'black'.

The advertisement could be as shown in Figure 6.1.

Part-time waiter/waitress to join
our friendly team at the White Hart.
No experience necessary
Own transport essential.
Phone Sara Smith on 00000 000000
between 9 am and 11 am

Figure 6.1 A typical staff advertisement

Qualifications

The majority of jobs in the licensed trade have not traditionally been related to formal training and qualifications. Waiting staff, bar staff, cellar staff, kitchen assistants and cleaners all tend to have acquired their skills by working at the job. S/NVQs (Scottish/national vocational qualifications) have been introduced to encourage staff to attain a set standard of basic skills and achieve a recognized qualification. The intention is that the variety of jobs in the licensed trade will increasingly be held by those with S/NVQs, thereby raising the status of staff throughout the industry and improving its professionalism. The scheme is run by the Hospitality Training Foundation (HTF).

It is fair to say that setting up the systems, training, monitoring and assessments for S/NVQs both for licensees and staff has not proved easy, even for the larger companies. Much progress has been made but there is still a great deal of work to be done.

Apart from the HTF's training division, the Hotel and Catering Training Company (HCTC), there are further education colleges and universities and a number of private training organizations which provide training courses leading to one of the recognized qualifications.

Many innkeepers understand the value of encouraging their staff to gain a formal qualification, not just for the sake of attaining the certificate but for the pride in the job which is thereby engendered.

The interview

Selecting staff is one of the key roles in any business and should be carried out by the innkeeper himself or herself. The interview is important for you and the candidate – take care in setting it up.

1 Give a clear brief about the time, venue and likely duration of the interview.
2 Hold the interview in an appropriate place where the discussion is not subjected to distractions and interruptions.
3 Set out for yourself in advance what attributes, skills and restrictions you consider (a) essential and (b) desirable. For instance, if you were interviewing for a waiter/waitress you may choose as follows:

Essential

- Cheerful, friendly
- Own transport
- Able to work Fridays and Saturdays
- Age eighteen plus
- No dishonesty in employment record
- Good health
- Will fit into the team
- Keen to learn

Desirable

- Some retail experience
- Able to work Wednesdays or Thursdays
- Age between twenty-five and fifty-five
- Live within three miles
- Keen to work extra shifts if offered
- Stable home background

4 Organize the interview by making sure you ask all the questions to give you the answers to 'Essential' and 'Desirable'.
5 Don't prolong the interview if you are getting all the wrong answers.
6 Write down the factual information to quote to likely candidates, e.g. working hours, dress requirements, rates of pay etc. (At the time of going to press the government is planning to introduce legislation for a minimum hourly rate of pay.)
7 Encourage the candidate to talk – you will only find out about him or her by listening.
8 At the end of the interview tell the candidate what happens next: 'I will phone you by Friday to tell you whether you have the job'. 'I shall take up the reference you have given me and be in touch as soon as possible afterwards'. 'I have enjoyed talking to you; subject to your references could you start on Friday week?
9 If it is a likely candidate give him/her a quick view of the dining room/kitchen/bar.
10 Make brief notes on each candidate immediately after the interview for your own guidance in making your response.
11 Take up references. Write to or, better still, talk to former employers. Much can be learned from such a conversation: listen for what is not said as well as what is said about the candidate. Honesty, or the lack of it, is often a subject employers hedge around.
12 Write to confirm offer of employment, covering the key points. See Figure 6.2.
13 Conclusion. If all this seems a great amount of trouble for one member of staff remember that your customers see your staff as an expression of your own management style: if the staff fail it is you who have failed in your customers' eyes.

A contract of employment exists between employer and employee as soon as an offer has been made and accepted, even verbally. It is wise to confirm the offer in writing. See also Chapter 11 on employment legislation.

The White Hart
Much Eating
Midshire

25 July 1999

Mrs J Jones
48 Somewhere
Much Eating

Dear Mrs Jones

Following our meeting yesterday, I am pleased to confirm the offer of employment as part-time waitress at the White Hart starting on Friday, 3 September. The hours will be 7 pm to 11.30 pm each Friday and Saturday, subject to variation by mutual agreement. The number of hours in any one week will not exceed xx and the hourly rate is £x.xxp.

Notice to terminate this employment is one week on either side.

We look forward to your joining our team at the White Hart.

Please sign the copy of this letter to signify your agreement and return it to me in the stamped, addressed envelope provided.

Yours sincerely

Sara Smith

Figure 6.2 A letter confirming offer of employment

Structuring the interview

It is easy for an inexperienced interviewer to let an interview get out of hand with too much time spent on certain areas and not enough, or none at all, on others. It is worth having a time structure for your interview as a guide. See Figure 6.3.

This is not to suggest that all interviews are totally controlled by the clock but the interviewer needs a framework to operate within or adjust if special circumstances demand.

Flexibility

Every innkeeper has had the experience of standing in his bar or kitchen surrounded by staff kicking their heels on what is normally a busy night and asking the baffled question 'Where are all the customers tonight?'

The certainty is that there will always be this element of unpredictability in the licensed and catering trades so you need good planning and perhaps good luck to overcome the problem.

You have to make the best judgement possible on your staff needs, balancing the essential requirement to meet the expectations of your customers with the awareness of staff costs and their effect on your bottom line.

The greater degree to which you can introduce flexibility to your staff schedules the better – demarcation disputes are the last thing you want to see within the pub or inn. Staff who can double up are precious indeed: the waitress who can adapt to being a barmaid in an emergency, the cleaner who becomes a kitchen helper, the barman who can cope with a crisis in the cellar.

Equally valuable are staff who can react to a cry for help from the management: those who can stay on for that extra hour, who can work the additional shift, who can come in at short notice if someone is sick, even **not** come in if the expected rush has not materialized.

It follows that many innkeepers prefer to operate with a

Minutes	
1	Introductions, putting the applicant at ease
2	Brief outline of job on offer
5	Applicant's work experience
2	Reason for leaving last job
4	Specific qualifications of applicant
4	Applicant's personal circumstances, family background, commitments etc.
3	Fuller description of job and job requirements
3	How the applicant matches the job
2	The inn, how it works, its customers
3	View of kitchen, bar, dining room
1	Summary of 'what happens next'
30	Total

Figure 6.3 Time structure for a staff interview

number of part-time staff who are flexible rather than a full-timer working the same number of hours.

Adaptable management

It is also of prime importance that the innkeepers (most usually a husband/wife or man/woman partnership) are themselves the most adaptable workers in the inn. They should be able to turn their hands to every job, for three reasons:

1 so that they understand the demands and opportunities of the job and are therefore better managers of staff in that position;
2 to plan staff schedules knowing they can step in at any point to augment staff where there is greatest pressure;
3 they can stand in for any key member of staff who goes sick or walks out and the operation will still continue smoothly.

Training

The major pub operating companies, leaders in their field, place strong emphasis on training, which suggests that the individual licensee ignores training at his/her peril.

So what do you need to do to ensure you have competent staff?

Let us assume that the training will be carried out by yourself 'in house' or by a senior member of staff under your guidance. Most jobs in the establishment, with the exception of chefs, require skills that are important but not intrinsically complex or difficult to learn, given a certain basic aptitude.

To train cellar, bar or waiting staff, cooks or kitchen assistants must be within the capabilities of the innkeeper. But too often the basic training is ignored and a new member of staff is thrown in to flounder or sink without proper guidance to help him or her survive.

As the employer, you have already taken great care in selecting your staff; you must now be as careful in training them in the way you want them to work. Remember, the customers judge your proficiency on the evidence of your staff.

Take as an example the barmaid you have taken on: she has had some previous part-time experience. The training will split into six parts:

1 *Induction*: hours of work, style of dress and appearance, area of responsibility, relationship to other staff, house rules, to whom responsible, health and safety, fire regulations, policy on children in the pub etc.
2 *Instruction*: where things are and how they work, the till and cash handling, glasswasher, ice machine, beer pumps, soft drinks dispense, food-ordering system, stock replacement procedure, obtaining change for the till etc.
3 *Product information*: give briefing on the drinks you stock, particularly any with which she is unfamiliar. Emphasize the selling points of those products you are keen to promote.
4 *Prices and measures*: make sure all prices are clearly marked or listed and she understands the measure the price relates to. Explain the law relating to measures of draught beer and spirits and the measure you require to be used for wines by the glass, sherries, martinis etc. Take care over mixed drinks,

how they are made and how charged – pint of light and bitter, shandies, lager and lime, gin and vermouth, spritzers and so on. It can cost you dear if you only find out a month later that your new barmaid has been giving the customers, in all innocence, double the measure for half the price because of your lack of instruction.

5 *How to pour drinks*: which glasses to use for various drinks, when to offer a choice, how to pull draught beer, pour a bottle of Guinness, serve a gin and tonic, mix a Bloody Mary etc.
6 *Customer relations*: the critical elements are dealt with in detail later in this chapter under Customer Care.

Staff skills training – summary

On reading the six training stages we have listed, you may doubt our statement that the barmaid's skills are 'not intrinsically complex'. However, although there is a great deal of knowledge you expect your bar staff to have or to learn, each part of that knowledge is in itself not complex.

The secret for your training is to show by example, to explain not just tell, to give the 'why' as well as the 'how', to take it at the pace with which the member of staff can cope and which makes allowances for his/her existing skill level; write down information for the staff's guidance where practical; keep an eye on progress, monitor performance and give additional guidance, encourage the member of staff to ask questions about anything of which he or she is unsure; build a two-way relationship which brings the best results for you, your staff and your customers.

Apprentices

Sixteen- and seventeen-year olds may be employed in a bar if they are in a Modern Apprenticeship Scheme. (See Chapter 11, under 'Other employee-protection legislation'). In addition to the Pub Apprentice there are also schemes for the Chef, Restaurant, Accommodation and Fast Food Apprentices.

Selection of chefs

Innkeepers who have quality restaurants and employ chefs need to take special care. Chefs are well-paid and choosing a bad chef can be expensive in every way.

Firstly, the innkeeper must have enough knowledge of operating a kitchen and planning a menu that he or she can run the interview for a new chef with the confidence that he/she will not be conned or browbeaten.

Secondly, the most thorough interview must be followed up with careful checking of references; this is more important than with any other member of staff because your inn's reputation for good food can be made or broken by the chef you employ.

Thirdly, you must, if necessary, be able to run the kitchen yourself so that your operation does not come to a halt if you cannot find the chef you want immediately. But, assuming you have found a chef who fits in well with your inn and its style, you will want to hold on to him or her. Apart from pay and conditions, the chef is likely to be influenced by the degree to which his/her creativity is allowed to develop. It is in your interests to encourage this creativity provided that it is within the bounds you set for the kitchen's profitability.

Finally, there is the question of training. If you believe it is to your inn's benefit, your chef welcomes the opportunity and there are appropriate courses available, then training will be a contribution to higher standards, wider skills and ultimately greater profitability.

It is perhaps worth adding the footnote that when we write of chefs, we mean skilled, professional men or women who can run a kitchen, buy wisely and create original dishes. He or she is not to be confused with the person who cooks in the kitchen where the menu is based on pre-prepared dishes and vegetables that only need defrosting and heating to set instructions. These are valuable members of staff but they will not draw that special treatment we have reserved for chefs.

Customer care

Customer care had become a fashionable concept as the eighties boom came to an end and the recession of the late eighties and early nineties bit deep into the turnover and profits of large and small businesses alike.

The sufferings of the licensed trade have emphasized the importance of the customer. When money is tight and drinkers and eaters-out are thin on the ground, then those who are still spending are precious.

There is nothing new in the idea that 'the customer is king'. The skilled, professional innkeeper has always recognized that it is only the customer who pays the wages or creates the profits and that satisfying the target customers' needs better than the opposition does is the ultimate key to success. As we have seen in Chapter 4, there is a great deal involved in setting out your stall, creating your consumer proposition and making your pub or inn uniquely attractive to your market.

But, however appealing you make your buildings or products, you will not create a truly successful business unless you also offer the customer that additional element of welcome plus service which is the hallmark of the quintessential British inn.

It is something we all recognize when it's there and miss when it's not. It is the reason why some pubs are busy while others, apparently better equipped or more conveniently situated, are not.

The standards for customer care must be set by the innkeeper personally. If it is your inn you must dictate how customers are treated and you will set the best example.

People visit a licensed establishment for many and various reasons but it is a minority who go simply to quench a thirst or fill a stomach. More often the aim is social enjoyment: to meet friends, engage in conversation, play darts, share the experience of a meal, feel part of a lively atmosphere. Few people go to a pub or inn wishing to be alone or to be ignored.

The innkeeper's job is to ensure that every customer who crosses the threshold is made to feel welcome (except those who would clearly be disruptive of his target market).

The standards he/she sets for himself/herself are also those he/she sets for the staff. Let us look at some key areas.

The greeting

Nothing is worse for a customer than entering the pub or inn and standing in no man's land with no one taking notice of him or her. Whether at a bar, in a dining room or reception desk, he or she must be acknowledged quickly and appropriately. You should aim for acknowledgement within ten seconds: even ten seconds seems a long time when you are waiting. By acknowledgement we mean that the owner or member of staff (although he or she may be engaged with another customer or on the telephone) makes it clear that he/she knows that the customer is there.

A few words such as 'Be with you in a moment, sir' are enough to hold the customer's interest until he can be served, although if you keep him waiting for two minutes further you are likely to lose him.

The greeting a customer gets will vary according to the style of the house. 'Good evening, sir, what may I get you?' from the barman at the traditional inn; 'Good morning, ladies, the lunchtime specials are on the board over there, would you like a drink while you're ordering?' from the owner of the general local; 'Hello, Harry, how did the darts go last night? – Pint of lager?' from the tenant of the estate local.

The rule is that the customer should get served quickly and be greeted appropriately so that he/she immediately feels welcome and part of the life of the pub. The professional innkeeper has an in-built perception which tells him/her how to pitch the welcome to strangers, how to draw that delicate line between formality and friendliness. It is a difficult skill to acquire or teach to staff. To find that you have engaged a new member of staff who is a 'natural' in this valued art is a bonus indeed.

It is worth emphasizing here that no time is more important for greeting people than in your first days in your new pub. This is when existing customers and potential new customers call in to weigh up the incoming licensee. Some of them may not have been in the pub for years. The impression you give on that first visit will influence, for good or ill, how you are perceived as the new innkeeper. Get off to a bad start and it is hard to make up the lost ground.

Holding the customer

The drinker

The customers you already have are the easiest to sell the next drink to. They have already been welcomed, so make sure the welcome is continued. If they are on their own, make conversation; if they respond you can be certain that talk is one of the reasons for the visit to the pub. If you judge the circumstances are fitting, draw them into conversation with other customers.

Many a licensee has experience of a customer who has become a regular simply because, on the first visit, he/she was made welcome and introduced to like-minded people.

When the customer comes up for a second drink, he/she needs to be served as efficiently as before but this time the server has a subtle change of attitude: this is a more knowing transaction, no longer a stranger but someone whose choice of drink is known – not 'What may I get you, madam?' but 'Gin with ice but no lemon?' being sure to ask the question, not to presume too far on the customer's choice.

A rapport is now established between customer and staff; the customer is being treated as an individual and their needs are being catered for.

What if a foursome of customers is sitting at a table away from the bar? The well-organized licensee will ensure that a member of staff circulates in the seating area to clear tables, empty ashtrays, wipe spillages – and to take the opportunity to talk to customers; even a few words are enough to let people know that they matter, are part of the scene. And those who feel cared for are more likely to stay or to come back.

This may well be the right time to introduce customers to other products – 'Let me show you our evening menu'. 'Have you tried the new Australian wines on offer this week?' 'We shall be putting on a big barbecue next Saturday evening'.

These are ways in which the innkeeper is selling to the customers: it has to be done skilfully and tactfully without overt 'pushiness'. But the good landlord is not just there to passively accept orders, he/she should be actively marketing the pub and products to new and existing customers alike.

The diner

It is just as important to build a rapport with those eating in your establishment, whether in the bar or in the restaurant.

However, diners in a restaurant or dining area separated from the bar need special treatment. The very fact that the room in which they are eating is apart from the hub of activity and bustle which is the bar servery means that the customers may be exposed to that most dangerous of afflictions in an inn – a feeling of loneliness. It is the owner's and staff's responsibility to see that diners are protected from any such feeling, initially by the warmth of welcome then throughout the meal by attention to detail in service.

This covers everything from seating people comfortably, guiding them through the menu and wine list if requested, serving courses promptly (without snatching plates away as the last mouthful is consumed), making sure condiments, sauces, napkins and bread rolls etc. are present or offered before being asked for, clearing the table of used glasses or spillages quickly and unobtrusively, being relaxed and friendly but not familiar in the service that is given.

The waiter or waitress is giving the impression that these particular diners matter, that their enjoyment of the meal is paramount. There is a form of service in restaurants which is high-handed and arrogant where the waiter or waitress looks down literally and figuratively on their customers. There is also the inappropriately over-effusive or obsequious style of service: both are equally offensive to diners.

The owner or manager is seeking that perfect blend of service which is professional but friendly, efficient but relaxed, warm and welcoming. We all enjoy this quality of customer care when we receive it – it does not come about by chance, it is the result of skilled staff selection and training.

None of the basic services mentioned above is difficult but staff need to be told what you expect of them (which can affect the kitchen as well as waiting staff), for instance:

- tables to be checked over as fully laid up before diners are seated;

- once seated, diners to be asked if they would like a drink before their meal, even if they have had one already while waiting;
- if the order has not previously been taken, menus to be given to all diners immediately they are comfortably seated and any special dishes explained, and the wine list offered to the host;
- orders to be taken within five minutes or as soon as customers are ready;
- orders to be repeated back to the customers in confirmation;
- no-one to wait more than fifteen minutes for the first course;
- plates to be cleared within five minutes between courses;
- no-one to wait more than twenty minutes between first course and main course;
- wine to be kept topped up where appropriate and additional wine orders taken;
- customers to be 'sold' the sweet menu, coffees, liqueurs in a non-pushy way;
- staff to be friendly, helpful, cheerful at all times;
- diners to be asked if they are enjoying their meal in a way that invites comments, not in a mechanical parroted question;
- any problem immediately to be brought to the management's attention;
- when customers have paid their bill and are ready to leave, they are to be thanked for their custom and bade goodbye.

Even if the diners are enjoying a high level of service from your staff, most will appreciate the owner/manager visiting the table during the meal to exchange a few words and add to the welcome and care being offered. You will also learn a great deal from diners' reactions both to the quality of the food and to the service.

Eating out in licensed premises has become big business, from the humble ploughman's lunch in the local to the stage-managed evening in the American-style pub-diner. Quality of food is, of course, important but it is the combination of value for money with an enjoyable experience that most determines the customer's choice of venue.

Dress

The way you and your staff dress sends a message to your customers, favourable or not. Dress is part of your presentation, the face your pub or inn shows the public.

It needs to be appropriate to the house and consistent with your marketing approach. 'Appropriate' may mean black ties for waiters and white blouses/black skirts for barmaids in a traditional pub-restaurant or T-shirts and jeans for barmen in an estate local.

In the pub-restaurant you are saying 'This is the sort of establishment where we offer and expect a degree of formality. We are traditional, perhaps even old-fashioned, restrained and set high standards'.

The estate local is saying 'We are relaxed, informal, have the common touch, understand our customers' tastes, don't expect us to cosset you too much'.

The range of dress style between these two extremes sends out equally clear messages: you should interpret these messages and make sure your staff are dressed to fit into the ambience you are creating.

On a practical level, if you are supplying staff with uniform, you are not only making a statement but adding a cost to your overheads. If staff are wearing their own clothes, those clothes must be clean and tidy at all times when the staff are on duty. Recently, we visited a highly-regarded, traditional food-led inn which, unusually, has only young, male bar staff. The food and service were excellent but the barman's scruffy jeans produced a jarring note. It was the scruffiness, not the jeans, we objected to. Subsequently, we discovered the owner was on holiday – when the cat's away ...!

Customers' dress can also contribute to undermining the atmosphere, particularly in the traditional inn. The days when ties had to be worn by men in restaurants are largely past as greater informality in dress has swept the land but we would not expect to see bare-chested men or men in sleeveless vests in this type of inn. It is a matter of aesthetics and not offending the tastes of your regular customers – so it is good business to exercise a discreet control on the more extreme limits of dressing (or underdressing)!

Summary

With the market ever more competitive, the quality of your customer care is the edge you can have on your rivals. The quality of care is determined by the standards you set for yourself and your establishment. Your style is all important – it must suit you and your customers. Having established your target market, you must create a team which delivers the service standards you have set and continually monitor their efforts to ensure they remain at the right level.

Some aspects of customer care are common to all pubs and inns, others will vary according to the type of house.

It is the innkeeper's skill in pitching his/her standards at exactly the right levels, whether in the estate local or traditional inn, which creates the mood of hospitality to attract and keep customers and build a successful business.

7 Profit control

One of the principal reasons for running a pub or inn is to make money. There will be many other, and perhaps higher, motives but, without this one, you are not going to be around long enough for them to make much difference to you.

You could be highly popular with your customers, your kitchen could have a country-wide reputation, your beer could win a CAMRA prize but, unless you are also competent at converting turnover into net profit, your business is going to fail.

The vast majority of innkeepers will be paying rent or repaying a business loan or mortgage; keeping up these payments month after month creates pressure. In this chapter, we will try to explore some well-tried and simple control measures that will keep you profitable and hopefully keep your financial stress to a minimum.

We heard recently of a well-respected innkeeper, with twenty years' experience and a healthy turnover of over £500,000, who is in financial difficulties. One of the root causes for the problem was totally inadequate stocktaking procedures. You may quickly respond and say that his procedures cannot have been too bad for him to have lasted over twenty years. It is likely that his business had been extremely inefficient for all that time but it has only become a potential terminal problem since his rent was re-assessed to around 10 per cent of his turnover. It is quite possible that he was losing 5 per cent or more of his turnover but, as he was still making a reasonable profit in spite of this, he never made the time to improve his efficiency.

We are going to cover control under three main headings:

- stocktaking and stock control;
- cash discipline and control;
- bookkeeping and accounts.

Stocktaking and stock control

If you were a busy brewery area manager, looking after vastly too many pubs and only had time to look at three lines on the accounts of each, you would probably select:

- VAT-exclusive takings;
- total labour costs;
- gross profit percentage.

The chances are, if these three all look healthy, then the net profit may well look good too. This is clearly too simplistic and the area manager should have the number of pubs cut down to allow time to study the accounts in much more detail. It does, however, underline the importance to the business of these three elements and highlights the importance of stock control.

All innkeepers need proper stock control whether they are employing staff or working the pub on their own. To have good stock control you must first have an appropriate stocktaking system.

It is quite possible, especially if you are useful with computer programs, to do your own stocktaking. If you have a sophisticated EPOS (electronic point of sale) till system, then it will be even easier for you to carry out this role. It is not recommended, though, as a good stocktaker is likely to only cost around £750 a year (depending on the frequency of stocktakes) and will do the job much more efficiently and quickly than you can.

We will concentrate on wet stocks initially but the principles of wet and food stocks are basically the same with the methods of calculation slightly different.

You need a certain amount of key information from your stocktaker, as follows.

Surplus or deficiency

Having counted your stock on hand and deducted this from the sum of the deliveries made and the stock on hand at the previous stocktake, the stocktaker will be able to tell you what your sales should have been. He or she will assume that all sales have been made at the prices shown on your price list, none wasted, given away, lost or stolen. This will be called 'sales at selling price'. The next calculation will be to total the money taken through the till since the last stocktake and the figures will be compared with the sales at selling price as shown in Figure 7.1.

Sales at selling price	£20,000
Cash taken through tills	£19,000
Deficiency	£1,000

Figure 7.1 A cash deficiency

There could be dozens of reasons why your stock is deficient and some of them are predictable and legitimate. A house beer line cleaning allowance is one example of this. It will not actually save you any money but might make you feel a little better. There is always some beer wasted during the pipe-cleaning process. This can vary considerably as it is affected by the length of run from cellar to servery, number of beer lines, diameter of the beer lines and the percentage of cask-conditioned ale. If you have fourteen beer lines with an average of two pints in each line and clean once a week, your weekly loss will be over twenty-eight pints. The calculation, assuming an average selling price of £1.78 per pint and a four-week stock period, would be as in Figure 7.2. You will see that after allowing for pipe cleaning you still have the problem of an £800 deficiency. We will return to some of the possible reasons for this later in this chapter.

Sales at selling price	£20,000
Cash taken through tills	£19,000
Cleaning allowance	£200
Deficiency	£800

Figure 7.2 The effect of a cleaning allowance

Gross profit (GP) and gross profit percentage

Next your stocktaker will calculate how much of your takings are GP. We have excluded VAT from all the examples on the next few pages to enable us to illustrate the points we are making more clearly. In the next example, VAT has been removed from 'cash taken through tills' and from 'cost of sales' (see Figure 7.3). To get the GP cash (b) is deducted from (a). To get the GP percentage (c) is expressed as a percentage of (a). You will have noticed that the GP is expressed as a percentage of the selling, not the buying, price.

If there had not been the deficiency of £800, the figures would have looked as in Figure 7.4.

(a)	Cash taken through tills	£19,000
(b)	Cost of sales	£9,500
(c)	Gross profit	£9,500
(d)	Gross profit percentage	50%

Figure 7.3 Gross profit percentage

Cash taken through tills	£19,800
Cost of sales	£9,500
Gross profit	£10,300
Gross profit percentage	52.02%

Figure 7.4 Gross profit percentage without deficiency

GP percentage by product

The next set of important figures for you to look at will be the GP percentages for each of the product groups as shown in Figure 7.5. You can see, at a glance, that your biggest product group is only producing 48.5 per cent GP, and a move up or down will have a disproportionate effect on your overall GP. A move in crisps and nuts will only have a marginal impact on overall GP.

The vital lesson to be drawn from this is:

- always ensure that your principal selling lines are priced at a level that will not dilute your overall GP percentage.

To help you further, your stocktaker will produce sales, percentage of total turnover and GP percentage for each product that you sell. A shortened form would look as in Figure 7.6. The products and GPs used are for illustration only.

You will remember that the overall GP on the draught was 48.5 per cent but the individual products making up this group vary from 55 per cent for Harp to 35 per cent on traditional cider. The market does not allow you to charge just what you like for your wares but you can, to an extent, massage things to your own advantage. The first product you must consider is traditional cider. It is accounting for 3.75 per cent of your total sales but only producing 35 per cent GP. You should

	Gross profit (%)	Percentage of total sales
Draught beers	48.5	60
Bottled beers and ciders	49.5	8
Wines	55.0	9
Spirits and liqueurs	62.0	7
Soft drinks	70.0	10
Tobacco (excluding cigarettes)	15.0	2
Crisps, nuts and sundries	25.0	4

Figure 7.5 Gross profit percentage by product group

pose and answer the following questions before taking any action:

- Is the wholesale price too high?
- Is the retail price too low?
- What are competitors charging?
- Is the product necessary to the business?

You may decide that the product must stay but that you will purchase a similar brand at a cheaper price. You may decide to move the retail price up in one go so that you achieve a respectable GP as quickly as possible or perhaps to edge it up over a twelve-month period. You could take the view that your customers would convert to another product if you removed this one, or that you may antagonize your customers less by increasing the price and letting it find its own level of sales. What you cannot do is nothing.

	Sales (£)	Percentage of turnover	Gross profit (%)
Carlsberg lager	3,000	15.0	52.0
Harp lager	2,000	10.0	55.0
Stella Artois	1,500	7.5	45.0
Boddingtons bitter	1,500	7.5	47.5
Local bitter	1,000	5.0	51.0
Draught Bass	1,000	5.0	45.0
Bells whisky	500	2.5	60.0
Fred McBloggs whisky	200	1.0	65.0
Becks bottled	400	2.0	40.0
Baby tonics	50	0.25	75.0
Traditional cider	750	3.75	35.0

Figure 7.6 Gross profit percentage by product

- The business cannot stand a low GP product with significant sales.

The next area you may look at is the sales of the two standard lagers. Perhaps Carlsberg is a little more popular than Harp but is there more you could do to increase sales of the higher GP item? If customers ask for lager without stating a preference, then sell the one with the higher gross profit. When serving lager or bitter shandies, then use the lager or bitter with the better margin.

The Stella Artois lager and draught Bass are both showing low GPs. Is there room for getting their price up or are they too price-sensitive to adjust? Are there similar products on the market with a lower wholesale price? You may decide that you must stock these actual products and that you have no room for price manoeuvres. If this is the case, you should not be over-zealous in promoting their sales and hope that other products with a better GP start to take market share from them.

Currently, fashionable beers such as Becks enjoy high sales in many pubs and inns. Often though, the price is too low, as in our illustration, to make them worth promoting. When you introduce a new and fashionable drink, ensure that it is priced to give an above-average GP. Do not have the bar full of young people drinking lager straight from the bottle at 40 per cent GP; if the habit must persist, at least get 50 per cent plus out of it.

Around forty years ago, Babycham was launched in Shepton Mallet. The marketing was inspired but, equally important, the company set wholesale and retail margins high enough to make everyone want to sell it. It worked and made the Showering family millionaires. It is a lesson largely forgotten today.

- Only stock new, fashionable lines if the GP percentage or GP cash is better than average for that product range.

Some stocktakers have a system of colour coding products such as red for products that are too low on GP and blue for products that are especially profitable. So make sure that your stocktaker helps you identify the problems and the opportunities. If the stocktaker does not, or cannot, produce this type of detailed information, then you must find a more modern stocktaker.

Gross margin and volume

One of the problems of the 1980s and 1990s has been the increase in gross margins at the expense of volume. This hit first in the south of England but the north and other parts of Britain are now similarly affected. There is a real chance that the wholesale and retail prices of ales, lager and soft drinks and, to a lesser extent, wines and spirits have gone past the point where the paying customer believes them to be good value. Some of the independent pub operating companies have tried to address this issue by using their buying power to get discounts that allow them to sell selected beers at well below their normal price. This is a dangerous area for the individual innkeeper to enter. It certainly cannot be guaranteed that, if you reduce prices, volume will increase but you can be quite sure that your GP percentage will go down if you reduce prices. If you do decide to improve volume by aggressive reduction in prices, then do not leave it open-ended. Use phrases like 'while stocks last', 'for a limited period only' or 'for this month only'. You can always extend the period if it is working but revert to normal pricing if it is not improving volume.

Figure 7.7 shows the effect of pricing on gross margin and turnover. To get sufficient impact, prices would have to be reduced significantly and we have used 15 per cent in this example.

All figures are net of VAT and it is assumed that all prices have been uniformly reduced.

You can see that, unless people drink more or you attract more customers, then takings actually are reduced. An obvious point but one that is often overlooked. The illustration shows that, in order to do no more than break even, additional drinks

Original weekly bar takings	£2,000
Original GP 50%	£1,000
GP after price reduction 41.18%	£700
Takings after price reduction*	£1,700
Takings needed to break even	£2,428

*Assuming no volume increase

Figure 7.7 Effect of a 15 per cent price reduction on takings

Original weekly bar takings	£2,000
Original GP 50%	£1,000
GP after price reduction 48.5%	£970
Takings after price reduction*	£1,970
Takings needed to break even	£2,062

*Assuming no volume increase

Figure 7.8 Effect of a 15 per cent price reduction on one product

to the value of £728 have to be sold. The picture worsens if you take extra bar staff wages into account but improves if you have negotiated volume-related discounts with your supplier.

A better method and easier to justify is selective price reduction. If you reduce one beer or lager by 15 per cent, and this only represented 10 per cent of your bar takings, the figures would look like Figure 7.8.

This looks much easier to achieve but it is likely that customers will switch to the reduced price product and it could represent 20 per cent rather than 10 per cent of your future trade. If this happens, the figures start to get a little more difficult to justify (see Figure 7.9).

Original weekly bar takings	£2,000
Original GP 50%	£1,000
GP after price reduction 47%	£940
Takings after price reduction	£1,940
Takings needed to break even	£2,128

Figure 7.9 Typical effect of a one product price reduction on takings and gross profit

So takings have to increase by almost 9 per cent to allow you to discount one product by 15 per cent. It can work, and works well for some, but it is all too easy to lose control. So be very careful.

Causes of deficiencies and how to take corrective action

You still hear it said 'I don't have a stock problem and having regular stocktakes is a waste of money' or 'I have had my staff with me for years and I trust them completely'.

Many years ago, an innkeeper told an apocryphal story and it still seems valid today. He was single and managed a very busy pub with a friend he had known and liked since his schooldays. All went well until he started getting serious stock deficiencies and he laid off all staff and he and his mate ran the pub on their own. Very hard work but they managed it and the stocks were perfect. They started to take on more staff and, soon after they got back to a full staff complement, the stock problems re-occurred. He laid off staff, one after the other, until it was back to just the two of them again, at which point stocks returned to normal again. The whole story occurred a third time and, yes, you have guessed it, it was his trusted friend who was the culprit. A sad, rather cynical story but full of lessons for every professional innkeeper.

Stock does not disappear on its own and it has either been given away, wasted, stolen or not delivered in the first place. There is always a solution to every stock problem as long as the control procedures are in place.

Some examples of how ale and lager stock can be wasted:

- poor stock rotation causing products to become unsaleable or difficult to serve;
- cask-conditioned ales tilted incorrectly and too late;
- dirty pipes or faulty equipment causing fobbing at dispense point;
- over-length beer lines, especially on to beer engines;

- beer lines not insulated or sufficiently clean meaning that beer will have to be pulled through at the start of each trading session;
- beer foaming over at the dispense point as a result of carelessness;
- over-sized beer glasses being filled beyond the line;
- 'half-pints' being poured, unmeasured, into pint glasses;
- bottled beer glasses being used for draught.

The remedies to some of the problems are obvious but others may take a little effort to eradicate. For example:

- to stop carelessness at the dispense point, do not allow staff to throw beer down the sink. Get them to keep it and measure it at the end of the session to illustrate how much they have wasted;
- insist on measuring half-pints into pint glasses;
- ensure that bottled beer (over-size) glasses are separated from draught beer glasses.

There are other ways that stock can be lost which are dishonest rather than just careless:

- drinks being given away or sold cheaply to friends;
- customers helping themselves, when you are not looking, to beers or even spirits if the optics are within reach;
- drinks being taken by bar staff, waiting staff or even cleaners without payment being made;
- false claims of 'drinks in' where the barman will claim that the drink he has just poured for himself was bought earlier by a customer;
- customer 'drinks in' where Fred pays for a drink for Harry which Harry claims later. There is no problem if it is only Fred and Harry but becomes one if Tom, Dick and the rest start doing it. In the confusion caused many innkeepers and bar staff give away drinks being falsely claimed;
- a similar problem to drinks in is when bar staff, or even the innkeeper, says 'thank you, I will have 50p worth' but then helps himself to twice that amount (a stocktaker friend of

ours has found that, in extreme cases, this can account for shortages of over 2 per cent of turnover);
- spirits stored in the bar as standby for the optics smuggled out in shopping bags or in overcoat pockets.

To combat most of these, you have to be well organized, watchful and have firm procedures:

- do not allow 'drinks in'. If a customer buys staff a drink, then it must be taken there and then. You may decide that drinking alcohol whilst on duty reduces efficiency and increases the temptation to steal;
- ensure your bar layout is secure enough to inhibit customers helping themselves; a mirror placed strategically and optics well out of reach helps. Always know how many bottles of spirits and wines are in your bar, having a standard amount to make it easy for you to notice a missing bottle;
- if you suspect your cleaner is having a couple of warming tots of brandy early in the morning, before you go to bed put a mark on the label to show how full it is. If you want to be slightly more devious in catching your thief, take the bottle down from the optic, mark its contents with the bottle standing upright and then replace it.

Do find time, especially if you know you have stock problems, to stand or sit at the customers' side of the bar and watch and listen whilst apparently socializing with your friends. If the problem is more serious, then get a close and discreet friend to do the watching for you. Make sure your friend is fully aware of the price of each drink so that undercharging on rounds can be detected.

Not all your losses will come from the bar; they can certainly come from the cellar and kitchen as well. Losses in this way can quite literally be termed 'wholesale losses'. There always seems to be one or two bad eggs in every basket and, sadly, the draymen, who deliver your beer and other drinks, are no exception. There is only one person worse than a dishonest delivery man and that is the innkeeper who buys the stolen goods from him. Short deliveries will happen unless you are careful. Be overtly well organized and watchful and the 'bad egg' will find an easier nest. These are a few of the measures you should take to ensure you get your full delivery and to help avoid the innocent mistakes as well.

- Always check your deliveries in, however busy you are. Try to get your suppliers to deliver at a time when you can supervise it.
- Always check your cellar before the delivery and know exactly how many casks and kegs are in there. Put chalk marks on free-standing unbroached kegs so, if they inadvertently finish up back on the lorry, you will be able to identify them as yours.
- Request that all your delivery is unloaded into one spot before it starts to be put into your cellar. Check the dates on the cask and refuse to accept cask-conditioned ale that is much more than two weeks old or keg beer or lager much over a month old. Check the delivery against the delivery note and check the goods again after they have been put into the cellar.
- Always check your empties beforehand and check these against the amount credited on the delivery note.
- Ensure that your bottled beer and soft drink stocks are well organized so that you can count what is there and ensure proper stock rotation.
- Keep your wines and spirits in a secure lockable store and put this stock away yourself. Be very careful about letting anyone else have this key except during your holidays and, possibly, for your day off.
- Always check your final invoice against the delivery note and make sure you get full credit for your returned empty bottles.
- One final check that is worth doing is dipping your cask conditioned beers once they are on stillage. Although it is apparently rare, breweries do sometimes have problems with under-filled casks.

You could well get the impression from this that everyone is out to rob you. What you will find in practice is that being systematic, well organized and watchful will protect you from most of these unpleasant problems.

If, by some mischance, you do have a problem of this kind with your brewery or soft drink deliveries, then have a discreet word with the director in charge of traffic. You will find that your complaint will be taken very seriously indeed.

A stock deficiency is not always due to stock going missing and the following are some of the other most common causes:

- rounds of drinks being incorrectly totalled by bar staff;
- dishonestly under-ringing into the till with the bar staff pocketing the difference;
- products incorrectly priced;
- incorrect measures being used such as Pimms priced at one sixth gill being sold through one-third gill 'vermouth' measures or 125 ml wine being free-poured into a larger glass;
- price increase on a product not noticed.

Some of these problems should be picked up quite easily and a good stocktaker will help you with most of them.

Pricing drinks in round numbers helps the less numerate bar staff. Adding £1.50 to £1.15 to 25p is somewhat easier than adding £1.47 to £1.16 to 27p. Customers do tend to complain more when they are over-charged rather than under-charged. The type of till that you use can also help you in this respect.

As mentioned earlier, especially if you know you have a problem, watch your till and listen to the amounts requested from the customer.

Cigarettes and cigars do not produce very much gross profit but are always difficult to control. Cigarette machines are now widespread, mainly for this reason, but are not particularly popular with the customers who smoke. If you do decide to sell cigarettes from the bar, keep the number of brands low and always stock the shelf yourself, keeping the balance in with your wines and spirits. Ideally, a separate till should be used for ease of checking. If this is not possible, either the money should be kept separately or, if rung into the bar till, a manual record kept. All rather long-winded but, if your staff or their family smoke, the temptation is very great. The innkeeper should do a quick stocktake daily and see if this tallies with the recorded sales.

The teenage children of the licensee have often been found to be the main culprits on shortages of cigarettes. It all underlines the attraction of cigarette machines where the owning company just gives you a share of 15p to 25p per pack sold, with none of your capital tied up in stock.

Dishonesty in the kitchen is perhaps more difficult to detect than in the bar. Many of the same principles apply.

- Check your goods in. It is easier to deliver one steak than one keg too few.
- Keep stocks as low as possible whilst ensuring that your menu is not compromised.
- Control waste – a much more skilful job than controlling beer wastage and, as with greengrocers, much of the profit comes from keeping waste to a minimum.
- Make sure your food does not finish up in the homes of your kitchen help.
- Check that your portion control is in line with the original way you costed the meal.
- Ensure good stock rotation and that food is kept at the correct temperature; with food poisoning an ever-present potential problem, an innkeeper has to be totally governed by sell-by dates.
- Continually check prices, some of which may change daily; some innkeepers prefer a fixed price, even if sometimes it may be slightly higher, than an ever-changing one.
- Create a system by which you can ensure that the payment for the food finishes in your till and not in someone's pocket; this will vary greatly according to the style of operation. The best food control systems are based upon the food till. If you can afford to, get one that links directly to a printer in the kitchen. The innkeeper must know exactly how many meals are being served from the kitchen and the value of them. If your till is not capable of checking this, then you must use numbered bills. Treat your numbered billpads as security items and make sure that each number is accounted for.

The innkeeper's family eating from the business has some clear attractions. It does, however, blur the attempts at full control over stock and GP. As in the bar, you may have an off-sales list on which you will record products sold at take-home prices rather than at optic prices so with feeding yourself and your family. Do keep a note of all food used for your own consumption so that you can calculate your true GP and perhaps detect that you have a problem in your kitchen. How easy for dishonest kitchen help to take note of your taking food upstairs without recording it. They know that you cannot be keeping close control on your food stocks and will take advantage of that. Dishonesty thrives on slack procedures.

Rolling food-stock checks

This is a simple form of food stock control which the innkeeper can carry out weekly. It is not completely accurate as it assumes the level of stock is constant but gives a good indication of the GP trends. All sales figures shown in the following example are exclusive of VAT. The GP percentage is arrived at by taking (a) from (b) and expressing it as a percentage of (b) as shown in Figure 7.10. The illustration shows that, once the ordering and sales pattern has settled down, the GP percentage remains reasonably constant. If there is a problem on pricing or pilfering, then the figures would not identify it as quickly as by taking a full weekly or monthly stocktake.

Keep stocks as low as possible as this will make checking quicker, pilferage easier to spot and reduce your chance of wastage. Keep a close eye on pricing and, if you are serving fresh foods, try to use foods that are seasonal and competitively priced.

Cash discipline and control

You cannot have good cash discipline and cash control without a lot of hard work. There are few shortcuts although a good till, appropriate to your turnover and needs, makes it easier for you.

There are only three places an innkeeper's cash should be:

- in the till;
- in the safe;
- in the bank.

Week	Purchases for one week (c)	Purchases running total (a)	Sales this week (d)	Sales running total (b)	GP (%)
01	1,000	1,000	1,500	1,500	33.3
02	800	1,800	1,600	3,100	41.9
03	700	2,500	1,700	4,800	47.9
04	800	3,300	1,600	6,400	48.4
05	700	4,000	1,700	8,100	50.6
06	700	4,700	1,500	9,600	51.0
07	800	5,500	1,600	11,200	50.9
08	800	6,300	1,600	12,800	50.8
09	900	7,200	1,700	14,500	50.3
10	700	7,900	1,800	16,300	51.5

Figure 7.10 A rolling food-stock check

Good cash control starts with always knowing how much cash you have. If you do not balance your cash on the first day, it will be twice as difficult to balance on the second. If you find a problem, it will be that much more difficult to pinpoint when and how the problem originally occurred.

In a busy inn with two bar tills and a separate till for food, a typical day in cash-checking terms could be something like this:

10 am — Prepare floats for the three tills. Take the till drawers to the room with the safe, close and lock the room door and count out each float. The float will normally be of a standard amount but should have sufficient £10 and £5 notes and £1 coins as well as smaller change to ensure that early customers proffering £20 notes do not cause you embarrassment.

10.30 am — You may have decided to bank each day and use the bank's night facilities at the weekend. In this case, having made up your floats for the morning session and assessed how much you may have to pay out to suppliers that day, you will pay the surplus cash into the bank.

3 pm — Remove all three till drawers and take a till reading. Take the drawers to the safe room and, having locked the door, count the cash in each till drawer and, having deducted the float, compare it with the till reading. If it is a few pence or a pound or so up or down, you may consider this reasonable. Record both the cash and the till reading in your till book showing the surplus or deficiency. Having counted and recorded all three tills, then prepare floats for the evening session, put them into the drawers and put the drawers and morning's takings into the safe.

At the end of the evening session, the whole cash-checking process will start again. You may decide to check your cash in the morning but it is better to do it before retiring for the night. Remember to leave the tills, minus their till drawers, open and to ensure that all cash and the till drawers are in the safe.

The final part of your cash check will be to record the day's takings less any cash payments and bankings made on your takings sheet. The balance should clearly equal the cash on the premises.

Tills

Your choice of till as an innkeeper must be determined by asking:

- What do I want this equipment to do and be?

The answers may include:

- be easy for me and my staff to use;
- record each transaction done;
- give me takings' totals by session, by day and by week;
- to fit an allotted space;
- offer reasonable security;
- affordable.

If these are the extent of your needs, you should purchase a straightforward electronic till with no frills. You would be able to purchase a new one of these for less than £350 and second-hand for around £100.

If your needs are a little more sophisticated such as:

- to enter products rather than cash,
- to assist you with stock control,
- to avoid mistakes on addition,
- to be able to run a check on sales of a certain product,
- to record food sales by dish,

then you will need a preset style of electronic till which is likely to cost you up to £1,000 each but, again, good second-hand equipment can be picked up for a few hundred pounds.

If your needs include the following:

- to be able to access the information from another location,
- to be able to link the tills to a remote printer in the kitchen or office,
- to monitor product groups and control stocks,
- to monitor sales by individual members of staff,
- to monitor sales by hour throughout the day or night,

- to link into a centralized computer,
- to have full use of information technology,

then you do need EPOS. It is expensive and will cost you £2,500 upwards per till plus printers and monitors. It is unlikely that this investment will be worthwhile in a pub or inn taking less than £250,000 a year.

A danger that has also become increasingly apparent is that the operator may start to rely totally on the EPOS system for the control and security of the business and therefore eases up on other control checks. There are always people who will delight in finding ways to get around the most sophisticated control equipment and an EPOS system in their hands, without other checks and safeguards, could leave you in financial difficulties.

A till must earn its keep by:

- enabling you to control or eradicate staff dishonesty or carelessness;
- giving you sufficient management information to enable you to run your business efficiently;
- giving you appropriate information for the size and potential of your business.

The choice of tills is wide; if you are replacing yours, make sure you see all the appropriate models demonstrated and fully understand what they can or cannot do. If possible, ask to see your chosen model in action in a busy environment and talk to the operator before you finally put your signature on the cheque.

If you are buying several tills and installing a brand new system, you are, as you will have already noted, making a major investment. Move with caution because your capital is precious and it is all too easy to be outmanoeuvred by a salesman or dazzled by technology.

There are many pubs and inns where huge investments have been made in EPOS where a simple till was all that was needed. There is no sadder sight to a pub-lover than seeing innkeepers poring over their information technology in some remote office whilst the customers are suffering from lack of attention at the bar or in the restaurant.

Cash checks

We have already stressed the need for firm cash management with cash checked and balanced each day or, better still, each session. If your tills are not balancing, it is likely that you have a problem. If they are over, it is often just as much of a problem as being under. You or your bar staff are either making innocent mistakes in change-giving or your staff are pocketing some of your cash. If you are having stock problems as well, then the till discrepancies could also be a clue to these.

Really dishonest bar staff often use a method of underringing the till throughout the session, estimating how much they will take out later, be it £10, £20 or even £50. They find it safer to build up the amount they are intending stealing and take it out later in the session when there is more money in the till. A cash check midway through the session could get results.

Take a till '*x*' reading before the start of the session; make sure your till is accurately floated; have a spare till drawer already floated and locked in your safe and then choose your moment to do your check. It is all very simple and your customers will not even notice what you are doing. You just arrive with your new till drawer, take a further '*x*' reading and take the original till drawer away to count it. If the problem has previously been serious, then a witness, other than your spouse, should check the original float with you, your '*x*' readings and the actual cash in the till. In this way, you will be better able to take disciplinary or even legal procedures against the offender, assuming of course there is one.

If the problem has been a major or a longstanding one, then it may pay to set the scene more carefully. Perhaps tell the bar staff that you will be out at the cinema and will not be back until closing time. If there is a thief, this should give the opportunity needed. All you have to do is to come back early and do a check an hour before closing.

Counting the meals

It is often easier to steal from the food operation than the bar, especially if kitchen and waiting staff are conspiring together.

It is all too easy, without a good food till and tight procedures, for staff to fail to ring into the till money taken for food. Use numbered billheads for each customer and make sure they are always used. Get a friend to check the number of meals served and ordered during a period when you have announced that you will be away from the premises. Check the bill pad numbers before leaving and check them again on your return. Check to see if the recorded number of meals served coincides with your friend's tally. Do it quietly and only say what you have done if you have uncovered a discrepancy. A degree of guile and covertness is needed with all these types of procedures. There is not much point in upsetting the innocent or alerting the guilty prematurely.

Accepting cheques and credit cards

Although some innkeepers have resisted, most have acknowledged the need for accepting credit cards for meals or accommodation. They are expensive, up to 3.5 per cent of the docket value is charged by the credit card companies to smaller traders, but there are many benefits. As long as you do not exceed your 'floor' limit without authorization and check that the signature tallies, then you will get paid. Customers paying by credit card seem to be more likely to be more extravagant than those paying in cash. The procedure is simple and efficient and it leaves less cash on the premises, reducing the risk of burglary.

It is relatively cheap to get on-line with the credit card companies with their PDQ (Pretty Damn Quick) machines. Visa and Access transfer the cash into your account within a few days so they are better for cash flow too.

Cheques are often a problem. Payment for meals by cheque, supported by a valid banker's card, is less of a problem than cashing a 'small cheque' as Peter Sellers in his famous thespian guise used to say. In both cases, look carefully at the banker's card, make sure it is in date and in the same name as on the cheque and that the signatures tally. Always write the card number on the back of the cheque yourself. As a routine, do not change cheques for strangers but, subject to the above, accept them from them in payment of their lunch or dinner bill.

Banking

At the time of going to press, the clearing banks are usually offering up to one year's free banking to new businesses. The cost of an inn's business banking account is now quite substantial, in a busy pub as much as £2,000 a year. It pays therefore to shop around and find yourself the best available deal. Banking cash and obtaining change is an expensive pastime and there is considerable merit in being self-supporting on change and in paying suppliers in cash; make sure, though, that you get a proper receipted invoice or bill at the time of payment.

For accounting purposes, it is preferable to have a business and a private bank account. This helps your accountant keep tabs on your business expenses and keep an eye on your cash flow needs. If you have several monthly bills that are not part of the business, it will help your bank charges to ensure that these come out of your private account, having first transferred the full amount in one transaction from your business account.

You should also open a business reserve account on which you will receive interest. The first purpose of this account is to hold the VAT you have collected pending payment to Customs and Excise. Secondly, to receive any extra account balance from your business account. There is little benefit in leaving excess money in a business current account.

Value added tax (VAT)

VAT is paid quarterly with the actual payment being made up to one month after the end of the quarter. In a mainly cash business like an inn, this means that you always will have money belonging to Customs and Excise. In a pub or inn doing £3,000 per week, this could amount to as much as £5,000, or an even greater sum in a quarter if food accounts for much more than 50 per cent of your business. It is prudent, therefore, to put around 10 per cent of your takings each week into your business reserve account. The 10 per cent is not precise and experience will show whether you have allowed too little or too much.

The principle of VAT is that you buy a product for a price plus VAT and sell it for a higher price plus VAT. A simple illustration is as follows. Purchase a case of wine for £100 plus £17.50 VAT. Sell the case of wine for £200 plus £35.00 VAT. VAT owed: £35.00 minus £17.50 = £17.50. The VAT owed is 7.4 per cent of the £235 selling price.

There is currently no VAT on the cost price of most food items and therefore the VAT charged with the selling price is owed to Customs and Excise. So, if your inn has a high proportion of food sales, you may have to reserve up to 15 per cent of takings.

You will find your local VAT office helpful and efficient. They are usually quick to repay money owing when VAT on purchases exceeds those on sales. VAT quarterly forms appear like clockwork in ample time for the return to be made. Customs and Excise are very strict on receiving payment on time. VAT for the three months ending 31 March must be with them by 30 April at the latest. They make the case, quite reasonably, that VAT is not yours to spend and therefore there can be no excuse, especially in a cash business, for late payment of it.

There is a temptation to use VAT for short-term borrowing purposes; do try to resist it – it can be a dangerous path to tread.

Amusement with prizes machines (AWPs)

We have already suggested that machines fit better into some types of pub than others. Having reached the decision that you will be installing a machine, it is very important that you manage it effectively. There is little point having a machine take up valuable space if it is not earning you profit.

How do you attempt to optimize your machine's performance? As we have written earlier, the big pub-operating companies employ resident experts to ensure that there is as much

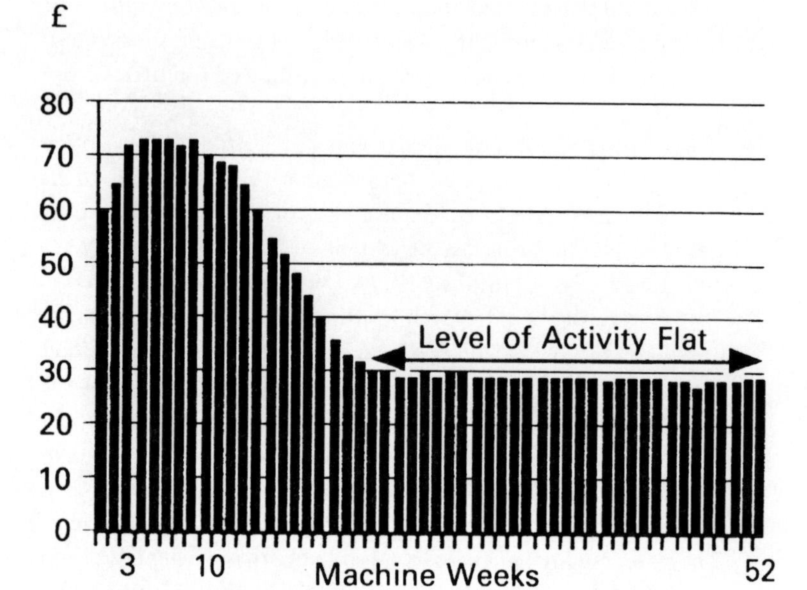

Figure 7.11 Typical AWP income cycle

profit as possible in each and every one of their machines. We were speaking recently to John Painter of JP&A of Reading. He is one of these experts and has started sharing his knowledge with individual licensees by publishing *What Amusement Machine?*

The typical AWP income cycle graph shown in Figure 7.11 is invaluable in understanding how machines perform. The graph shows that when a new model machine goes into a pub or inn for the first time:

- income tends to rise as players get to know the features;
- after just three weeks, the initial interest wears off and the curve starts to flatten;
- from about week 10 onwards, the income starts to go into steady decline;
- the decline flattens out to around 40 per cent of the peak.

John makes the point that many individual licensees are in the flat activity area and, as they do not see much change in the machine income, do not ask for a different machine. They usually have inadequate records and, as a result, have low income expectations.

The 'ripple effect' of machine changes

The graph in Figure 7.12 shows how, by anticipating serious decline in a machine's takings, the income from it could double. What you need to do is to keep weekly records of income and wait to note any decline and then quickly arrange for a change of machine. This process is repeated when the income from that machine too starts to decline and so on. Although this is normally around thirteen weeks, you should not automatically change unless it starts to decline. If it is still earning good money, stick with it a few weeks longer.

- John Painter believes the 'ripple effect' is fundamental to maximizing machine income.

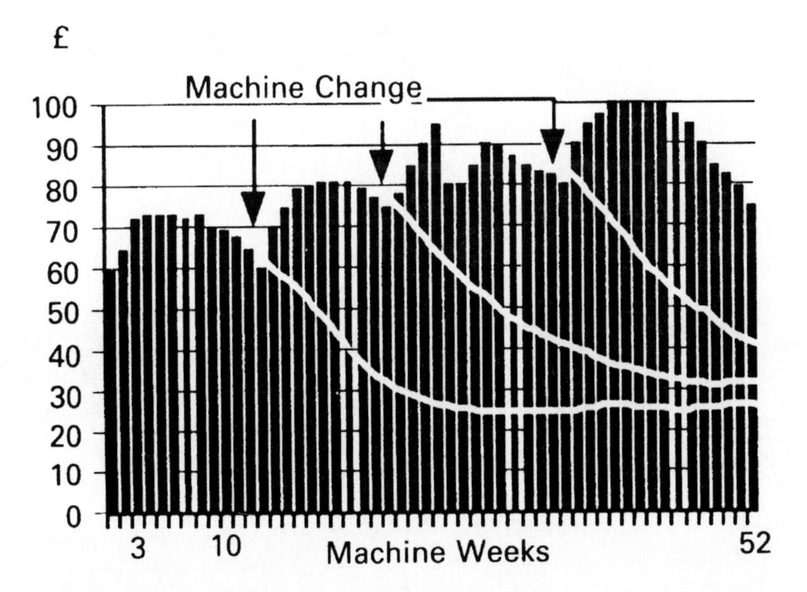

Figure 7.12 The ripple effect of machine changes

Before leaving AWPs, it is worth mentioning the machines themselves. There is no point, in a fast-moving business like amusement machines, quoting makes and models in a book such as this. You should, however, take note that, of the fifty-two machines reviewed by John, only ten were described as excellent, seven as good and a massive thirty-five adequate or poor. There was no particular correlation between machine rental and performance.

Accountancy and bookkeeping

There is not space in this book to show the basics of bookkeeping and accountancy. What we are trying to illustrate are the reasons for good record-keeping and the need for accurate, useful financial information.

In the days when trade was buoyant and rents were low, the average innkeeper felt they needed simple records and some end-of-year accounts. It was not unusual for innkeepers, through various inefficiencies, to lose 5 per cent or more of their takings because of poor control. With brewery leasing departments using computer models for rent assessment purposes, the Inland Revenue using managed house information to establish 'norms' for the business and Customs and Excise potentially able to charge VAT on stock shortages, there is a clear need for a more professional approach.

Takings books or sheets

The example in Figure 7.13 is a typical modern way of manually recording business done. For those with in-house computers, this type of record is superfluous but, for the majority, it will do the job. It includes the discipline of checking takings and therefore cash twice daily. It also forces the user to balance the cash on a daily basis.

			Sunday		Monday		Tuesday		Wednesday		Thursday		Friday		Saturday		Total	
	Opening Balance		1205	79	1797	86	618	48	792	85	733	79	751	83	823	29	983	08
	Wet	A.M.	185	31	85	25	79	27	103	15	85	73	116	19	82	38	737	28
		P.M.	120	16	152	11	168	77	211	11	262	18	403	70	467	19	1785	22
		Total	305	47	237	36	248	04	314	26	347	91	519	89	549	57	2522	50
I	Catering	A.M.	291	85	75	10	81	73	68	05	51	70	135	73	55	87	760	03
N		P.M.					52	15	73	58	100	90	230	55	361	90	819	08
C		Total	291	85	75	10	133	88	141	63	152	60	366	28	417	77	1579	11
O	Other	A.M.																
M		P.M.							27	90							27	90
E		Total							27	90							27	90
	Total Takings		597	32	312	46	381	92	483	79	500	51	886	17	967	34	4129	51
	Machines						167	53									167	53
	Other										5	80					5	80
	Total		597	32	312	46	549	45	483	79	506	31	886	17	967	34	4302	84
E	Cash Payments		5	25	138	58	375	08	103	90	38	27	212	90	153	70	1027	68
X	Drawings														350	00	350	00
P	Bankings Cash				950	00			363	15	450	00			200	00	1963	15
E	Bankings Visa				265	17			75	80			105	37			446	34
N	Bankings Access				138	09									103	85	241	94
S	Net Wages												496	44			496	44
E																		
S	Total		5	25	1491	84	375	08	542	85	488	27	814	71	807	55	4525	55
	Closing Balance		1797	86	618	48	792	85	733	79	751	83	823	29	983	08		

	Gross		PAYE		Pension		Ees NI		Oth Dedn		NET		Ers NI		Ers Pensn	
Weekly Wages	549	50	34	70			18	36			496	44	21	41		

signed Glyn Jones

Figure 7.13 An example of a completed weekly takings sheet

Annual forecast

Some accountants will supply you with monthly or quarterly management accounts. These are an important instrument for controlling your business, especially during its formative years. They are, however, fairly meaningless unless they link into a forecast of the income and expenditure that you produced before the start of the year or before taking on the new business. An example of a forecast is shown in Figure 3.8 as part of the business plan. This type of document is produced by computer but is designed to keep the number of expenditure lines down to a minimum. You could have a line for toilet rolls, furniture polish, the pipe cleaner and so forth but it is easier to get a clearer picture if these are all grouped under 'hygiene'. When the original forecast was done, there was a computer line code for each of these items and your accountant should be able to give you a full breakdown on 'hygiene' if you need it.

It is vital, when preparing a forecast, that estimates of income are not over-optimistic. Equally, it is dangerous to set yourself expenditure targets that are unrealistically low. If you are expecting higher food takings, for instance, it is most likely that wages will need to move up as well.

Monthly and quarterly management accounts

These are at their most useful when they are compared with forecasts and with last year. If, before taking a pub, you have produced a business plan showing a certain level of income, it is vital that this can be measured from the start. You must know if your takings are in line with your plan and, if not, you must attempt to boost them or reduce the expenditure. It always strikes us as most unsatisfactory when an accountant, a full fifteen months after a business has started, produces accounts saying 'Sorry, old chap, but you seem to have had a poor first year'. To run a business professionally, you need accounts that help you manage the operation week by week, not just a record of historical takings and expenditure. Figure 7.14 is an example of management accounts which must be easy to read and should be capable of highlighting problems. Management accounts allow you to take action early so that problems can be tackled and opportunities capitalized upon.

Takings and costs in harmony

As a generality, large managed houses are often good at controlling costs but less proficient at generating takings. Many entrepreneurs, in tenancies, leases or their own freeholds, tend to work very hard on building up takings but sometimes spend too little time on controlling costs.

A combination of the best of both will give the innkeeper a profitable future.

It is very easy to pay your employees a little too much per hour or to have them on duty for more hours than is necessary. Plan staff to come on at intervals. It is wasteful having four bar staff on at 5.30 when trade only warrants two up until 8 pm. You do not necessarily get the best staff by paying more than your competitors. It can be much better to improve the quality of their working environment, by good training, plenty of verbal recognition when a job is well done or by making your place fun to work in.

Prepare a specification of works for your cleaners so that everything is cleaned when it needs cleaning. There is no point having a cleaner clocking up hours cleaning items daily which can equally well be done weekly. If you go to the trouble of producing a detailed specification, you can also check that everything is being cleaned to your satisfaction. Take care that cleaning materials are not wasted or misused as the cost of these can be significant over a year.

A way of building trade is by generously treating customers to drinks or even snacks. If this is working well for you, then set yourself a forecast of the cost and stick to it. Often, it does not really increase trade and is a direct drain on profits. Although you may find it painful, set a limit on this spending and keep to it.

Many of the larger costs such as rates, rent and mortgage repayments cannot be controlled. This makes it imperative that you keep a tight grip on all costs that are controllable.

Current Period					Year To Date			
Actual	%	Vnce to Budget	Vnce to Last Year		Actual	%	Vnce to Budget	Vnce to Last Year
13,621	92%	1,121	1,500	Wet Take	39,221	93%	2,221	5,001
1,157	8%	357	670	Catering Take	3,005	7%	205	1,700
12	0%	12	10	Other Take	12	0%	12	(36)
14,790	100%	1,490	2,180	**Total Take**	42,238	100%	2,438	6,665
420		(80)	(20)	AWP	1,200		(100)	(70)
265		(35)	(35)	AWOP	725		(55)	(74)
685		(115)	(55)	**Total Machine Income**	1,925		(155)	(144)
15,475		1,375	2,125	**TOTAL SALES**	44,163		2,283	6,521
6,689		564	810	Gross Profit Wet	19,199		1,251	2,719
602		174	407	Gross Profit Catering	1,555		71	1,098
697		(103	(45)	Other Gross Profit	1,937		(143)	(180)
7,988	54%	635	1,172	**TOTAL GROSS PROFIT**	22,691	54%	1,179	3,637

(1,250		0	(62)	Salary/Relief	(3,250)		0	(120)
(1,050)	–7%	14	(41)	Wages/Casuals	(3,160)	–7%	24	(125)
(123)		(23)	(11)	Contract Labour	(304)		(44)	25
(160)		2	(14)	NI/Pension	(420)		31	(60)
(2,583)	–17%	(7)	(128)	**TOTAL LABOUR**	(7,134)	–17%	11	(280)
(350)		(13)	0	Electricity	(928)		(53)	10
(145)		14	(10)	Gas	(395)		18	(66)
0		0	(5)	Other Fuel	0		0	(5)
(495)	–3%	1	(15)	**TOTAL ENERGY**	(1,323	–3%	(35)	(61)
(70)		80	(5)	Music/Entertainment	(331)		59	(25)
(35)		(10)	(15)	Utensils	(751)		14	(60)
(114)		11	10	Hygiene	(417)		(92)	(23)
(125)		(25)	24	Telephone	(280)		(20)	64

Figure 7.14 An example of a monthly management account

(682)		(107)	354	Repairs & Renewals	(1,679)		16	684
(82)		(7)	(15)	Transport	(200)		(5)	(6)
(5)		5	(5)	Bar Sundries	(30)		(4)	0
(41)		9	(11)	House Promotion	(280)		50	(15)
(174)		(24)	(23)	Sundries	(1,517)		(127)	(75)
(1,328	–9%	(68)	314	**TOTAL GENERAL EXES**	(5,485)	–13%	(109)	544
3,582	24%	561	1,343	**CONTROLLABLE PROFIT**	8,749	21%	1,046	3,840
(1,346)		0	0	Rent	(3,500)		0	0
(267)		21	(41)	Rates & Water	(701)		49	(120)
(98)		52	(12)	Bank Fees	(168)		222	(100)
(120)		10	0	Professional Fees	(421)		(31)	0
(250)		0	0	Depreciation	(650)		0	0
(41)		(1)	(2)	Insurance	(97)		7	11
(2,122)	–14%	82	(55)	**TOTAL FIXED EXPENSES**	(5,537)	–13%	247	(209)
1,460	10%	643	1,288	**NET PROFIT**	3,212	8%	1,293	3,631
49.11%		0.11%	0.61%	Wet GP %	48.95%		0.44%	0.79%
52.03%		–1.47%	12.03%	Dry GP %	51.75%		–1.25%	13.75%

Figure 7.14 *(continued)*

Energy conservation

Pubs and inns are heavy users of energy. They need lighting, both internally and externally, heat to the bars and the accommodation, fuel for cooking, often for several hours at a time. On top of this, there is smoke extraction from the public areas, extraction from the kitchen, cooling to the cellar and many pieces of heavy-duty equipment. Air conditioning in pubs is becoming, at long last, more commonplace but these units are also expensive to run.

The costs are large enough to make it worthwhile looking at conservation measures.

- Make sure you are on the best tariff for both electricity and gas supplies.
- Consider investing in low-energy lamps in service areas: these are expensive to purchase but will give you a steady payback in reduced electricity bills.
- If it is possible, try to get some form of porch so that all your expensive heat does not leak out of the door every time a customer comes in.
- Have a controllable heating system that can be reduced when the bar or restaurant fills up with customers. Customers are an excellent free supply of heat.
- Do not have a cooled section of your cellar that is too large for your turnover.
- Insulate not just roof space, but cellar ceilings, central heating pipes and hot water tanks.
- Even in an old inn, try to get your windows and doors draughtproof.

Finally, like so many of these matters, take expert advice before spending too much money on conservation. It makes the cost much easier to justify if someone can accurately predict the savings from a particular course of action. Perhaps you could even find yourself eligible for a grant for insulation from your local authority.

VAT accounting

Your accountants, if they are producing quarterly management accounts for you, can also produce, with little trouble, your VAT return. Although you could do this yourself it is usually a better use of time delegating it to your accountant or your personal bookkeeper.

End-of-year accounts and tax returns

You should always use an accountant for your end-of-year accounts. The rules on taxation are constantly changing and it is false economy to attempt to do it yourself. The Inland Revenue are very helpful and will take care to explain things to you as simply as possible. They are, however, like Customs and Excise, severe on late payments and unforgiving if you try to deceive. Self assessment was introduced for the first time in 1997 and fines of £100 are levied on late returns plus interest on any payments due.

Pay as you earn (PAYE)

As an employer, you will be deducting tax and National Insurance from your employees. There is no shortcut to doing it properly and, although people still talk of 'cash in hand' for wages, it is a shortcut to financial suicide. There are companies that will do weekly payroll for you, complete with payslips and tax computations. These cost as little as £15 per week and the time you save can be used in developing the business.

Cost of accountants

This varies greatly from around £500 for basic end-of-year accounts with you doing all the bookkeeping to £2,000 or more. Make sure you ask the price and exactly what the accountants will be doing for that price. Match the size of the accounting practice to your business: there is no point in engaging the services of a major national practice if you are taking £2,000 a week. You would be better served by a suitably qualified small local firm.

Private housing for innkeepers

If you are a lessee or tenant and have sold your house to enter the business, you could well be building up a longer-term problem for yourself. There was a lovely old couple who had sold their house to take a pub tenancy. They did an excellent job for over 20 years and apparently were quite profitable. In spite of regular savings and pensions schemes, they found that all the money they had made was insufficient to buy back the equivalent of the house they had previously sold. The moral is: do try to hold onto your private house if you possibly can but, if you cannot, then make every effort to start buying a house at the earliest opportunity. Although house prices fell in the early 1990s they recovered and most experts predict that the long-term trend is upwards.

Pension schemes

We are not qualified to give advice on pension schemes but, if you are self-employed, you will have to make your own pension arrangements. Do take independent advice. The principal benefit of pension schemes is that they are tax-efficient but the basic problem is that your money is locked into the scheme and unavailable for your use if your business gets cash flow problems.

Summary

In this long chapter, we have tried to highlight the basic principles of good profit control practice. We have stressed the importance of:

- tight and efficient control of stocks;
- detailed pricing with GPs for each product;
- getting the balance right between turnover and GP;
- cash and till control and cash checks;
- getting the costs and takings balanced;
- selecting the correct style of till;
- understanding the AWP 'ripple effect';
- cost-effective energy conservation;
- producing a forecast of business you expect to do;
- good topical financial information.

Taking money through the till is vital but, without common sense and discipline in all these areas, takings may not finish up giving you the profit that you are working so hard to achieve.

8 The perfect pint

Cellar management

To a newcomer to the trade, coping with the beer cellar often appears to be one of the most daunting tasks to tackle. In practice, it is not. The technology is simple, there are sources of advice readily available and the mystique is soon assimilated.

Nevertheless, having a reputation as a good cellarman is a key factor in almost any pub's success. When, in an average pub, 60 per cent or more of drink sales are draught beers, it is clear that serving a first-class pint is a skill the innkeeper has to learn, and learn well.

Even in a traditional food-led inn, where perhaps only 40 per cent of sales are drinks, the cask-conditioned ales will still be an important factor in influencing the customer's perception of the overall quality of the inn.

Sources of advice

Because it is in the brewer's interest that the beers are served to the public in prime condition, the brewery company will take pains to ensure that a licensee who lacks experience will be offered advice and training. This may be carried out in a brewery training school as part of a wider course or as a one-off. In either case, a half-day's training supported by a simple cellar management booklet and fault-finding guide is normally enough to set the licensee on the right track.

Tenants or managers of tied houses should get the necessary training from the parent brewer; owners of free houses will find that among the various brewers competing for their trade, there will be those only too eager to throw in a training package to try to win the business.

Installations and loans

In a cellar, there is all or some of the following equipment designed for:

- storing beer (casks, kegs, stillages),
- cleaning beer lines (cleaning ring main, cleaning bottles),
- raising beer (CO_2 cylinders, mixed-gas cylinders, gas lines),
- temperature control (cellar cooling/warming installation, remote beer cooling unit),
- hygiene (sink with hot and cold water; sump and sump pump – in underground cellars).

In a tenanted tied house, it will vary from brewer to brewer as to what the brewery owns and what the tenant owns and is responsible for. But a tenant who is showing that he or she can grow the trade has a good chance of persuading the brewer to improve his or her cellar to the benefit of them both.

The new tenant or lessee should certainly take the state of the cellar into account when negotiating the tenancy and try to squeeze as many cellar improvements as possible from the pub owner before signing up.

The free trader is in a much stronger position. He or she is continually courted by the brewers and thus has every chance of getting cellar equipment or cellar improvements from the supplying brewer. Equipment is usually 'plant on loan' which costs the licensee nothing and improvements are with low interest loans or loans linked to barrelage targets.

Either way, the free trader should be able to organize an excellent cellar at relatively low cost.

Basic rules

We began this chapter by stating that cellar management is not a complex matter. However, it is one where simple rules and procedures have to be followed every day, seven days a week because consistency and beer quality are the keys to success.

Hygiene

Walls, floors and ceiling must be sound, readily washable and clean. Beer is a 'live' product and is susceptible to infection from airborne bacteria. Cleaning must be thorough and frequent with beer spillages wiped up immediately.

Temperature

The recommended cellar temperature range is 55–60°F (12–15.5°C) although many brewers prefer a top figure of 58°F (14.5°C). Keeping beer at a consistent temperature is fundamental in maintaining quality: below 54°F (12°C) there is the risk of a 'chill haze' on cask-conditioned beers and loss of condition, above 60°F (15.5°C) and you are likely to get excessive fobbing. In either case, the customer will not appreciate his or her 'real ale' at too low or too high a temperature.

Cellar temperature-control systems are often referred to as 'cellar coolers' but it is important to remember that too cold a cellar can do as much damage to beer as too warm a one.

Keg beers (lagers, brewery-conditioned bitters and milds, stouts) also benefit from the correct cellar temperature although many are further chilled by going through a cooler prior to dispense (as are keg cider and draught soft drinks).

However, particularly in those pubs catering for drinkers where lagers and smooth-flow bitters predominate, temperatures are kept markedly lower, even as low as 3° centigrade. The vogue for colder and colder drinks usually pleases the younger drinker although it is anathema to the more traditional customer.

It is not unusual to find ice machines or in-line beer-cooling equipment sited in the cooled part of the cellar. It is very inefficient use of energy to have heat-generating equipment working against the cooling system. As long as space permits, keep all other equipment out of the cooled section of your cellar.

Beer line cleaning and routine cleanliness

Beer lines, if left unattended, soon accumulate a yeast deposit which restricts the flow, causes problems with dispense and affects the taste of the beer. Lines must be thoroughly cleaned once a week using a recommended solution. Modern cleaning ring main systems make this a far simpler and quicker task than it once was.

Beer taps and keg connectors should be thoroughly cleaned between use and spiles ('hard pegs' or 'soft pegs') should never be reused.

Cask-conditioned ales

These ales need more loving care from the innkeeper than any other simply because they are 'live'; after the beer is delivered, secondary fermentation will take place in the cellar. The control of this fermentation is the cellarman's skill.

Casks should be stillaged if possible on delivery and the plastic tup replaced by a soft (porous) spile after about four hours thus allowing the beer to work. At the same time, the cask may be tapped. The spile needs to be regularly checked and changed if necessary – only when the beer has stopped working is the soft spile replaced by a hard spile. Leave the hard spile in for at least four hours to allow condition to build up within the cask. The beer will then be in condition to sell.

When you start to draw off the beer, you must remove the hard spile; this allows sufficient air into the cask as each pint is pulled, thus avoiding a vacuum being created and the beer being stirred up.

It is essential that the spile is replaced firmly between sessions or the beer will lose all its natural condition and appear flat and lifeless.

Before the cask is half-empty, slightly tilt the cask so that you draw all the good beer you can from it. Do the job carefully or you will disturb the 'bottoms' and make the beer cloudy. Avoid over-tilting as this will tend to bring the 'bottoms' around the area of the tap.

When a cask is empty, the tap must be removed from the keystone, the cask sealed and removed from the cellar.

An alternative to hard and soft spiles is the automatic beer vent which is a device designed to avoid the attention described above. However, it needs constant cleaning and our personal preference is for the 'hard and soft' system.

Some brewers allow, or even encourage, landlords to use what is called a 'blanket pressure' of CO_2 on their cask ales to help maintain condition. We are not enamoured of the system although it is a matter of personal judgement as to whether the taste of the beer is affected, particularly if only a very light 'blanket' of 2 lb of CO_2 is used.

Keg beers

These beers come in sealed containers and need no attention other than ensuring that the balanced CO_2 or mixed gas pressure at which they are dispensed is correct. The pressure gauges are normally set by the supplying brewery and should not be tampered with. If the pressure is wrong, the beer will dispense badly usually with an excess of fobbing. Interestingly, if a keg beer is fobbing at the dispense point, it is usually either that the temperature is too high or the gas pressure too low. Many less able cellar staff believe that **reducing** pressure stops fobbing. The other common cause of fobbing is dirty pipes so customers in the know tend to avoid pubs with fobbing beers.

Stock rotation

Cask and keg beers are delivered with a date stamp on them showing when they were filled at the brewery. It is important you use them in the correct order so that you are not left with old stock. Brewers give credit in certain circumstances for unsaleable beer but will not give it if the cask or keg is beyond their recommended sell-by date

Cask ales ideally should not be on dispense for more than three days. The quicker you sell it the better: by fitting a Y piece to the tap you can dispense to more than one beer engine in your servery.

Keg beers have a much longer life but even they will tend to over-carbonate if left too long on dispense.

It follows that you must adjust your ordering by size of container to allow for your turnover of particular beers: a slow-moving cask ale needs to be ordered in firkins (nine gallons), a higher-turnover lager in eighteen-gallon kegs or larger if your brewer supplies them.

Bottled and canned beers and minerals also have 'sell by' dates and stock rotation for these should be part of your system. Always pull stock forward and stack new stock behind the old. Do the same with the products on your shelves. Get into the habit and you will do it automatically, even when you are especially pushed for time.

Tidiness

A cellar should be tidy and well-organized not only for your greater efficiency but to avoid the risk of accidents. It should be used only for beer and not as a general food store for mushrooms, potatoes, lettuce or miscellaneous foodstuffs.

Lighting

Good lighting is essential, again to prevent the risk of accidents, particularly in underground cellars. Unlike in bars, fluorescent lighting is to be welcomed.

Layout

The cellar is a working area and needs to be planned. The nearer that kegs and casks are to the bar services, the shorter the beer lines and the less potential wastage. Cask ales on stillage need space for you to work with them and should be positioned where they are least likely to be disturbed. Cask areas and keg areas should be separated. Make cleaning around the containers as easy as possible. Keep beer lines tidy and off the floor. If you have the space, keep empty containers in a separate store.

CO_2 and mixed-gas cylinders

Great care should be taken with cylinders. They are filled under great pressure and, if they leak or blow out their safety valve, they could quickly fill the cellar with a deep blanket of unbreathable gas. They can be equally dangerous if carried in the back of a car, especially in hot weather; if one 'blows' it will instantly mist up the windows apart from being unbreathable. The third potential danger is their weight; they should always be stored lying down or fixed to a wall as one could easily break a leg or foot if it falls over.

See Figure 8.1 for a practical cellar layout.

Filtering back and beer mixing

It is legal to filter beer back into a cask provided that a proper filter is used in a hygienic way and only clean beer from the cask is put back into the cask that it came from. We are unhappy about this practice having known it all too often to be abused. The risk of affecting the quality of the beer is, we think, too great for the practice to be encouraged. The temptation is there for an unscrupulous or careless landlord or member

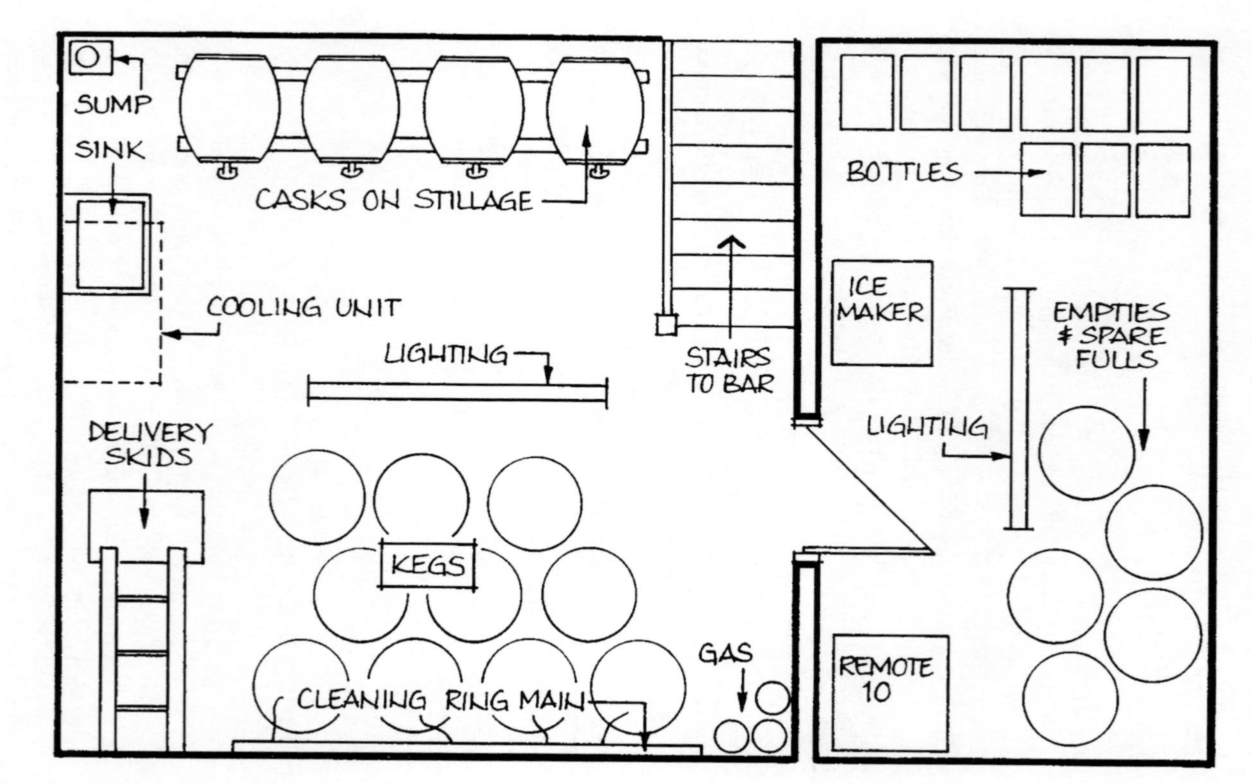

Figure 8.1 A typical cellar layout

of staff to filter back beer wrongly, and, for the sake of a short-term additional profit, this could damage the pub's reputation as a good beer house.

Mixing or diluting beers is clearly an offence which the Excise will treat seriously and could well lead to a publican losing his or her licence.

Beer-handling equipment

The beer handles prominent on a bar counter are seen as the symbol of a traditional pub in most parts of the country. The beer engine is the commonest form of dispense for cask-conditioned bitters and milds. But there are other forms of dispense: straight from the cask in the bar servery (creates an excellent image but difficult to control beer temperature and condition); by electric pump (where the distance from cellar to bar counter is too far for other methods to function effectively); by metered dispense (where the beer is measured in the cellar or at the tap so that an exact half-pint is delivered each time), and, the commonest for keg bitters, milds, stouts and lagers, the full pressure gas system with its familiar illuminated dispense taps ('fonts') on the bar counter.

In a cellar where space is extremely tight, the ale casks, instead of being stillaged horizontally, may be stood on their end and a vertical extraction system used.

In pubs with exceptionally high beer sales, the brewer may decide to install permanent tanks in the cellar and the beer is delivered in bulk. This is a system rarely seen in the south of England.

Changing fashions in beer types and dispense

As with every industry, the licensed trade has been subjected to fluctuations in fashion often led by the major brewers. In the years after 1945, it seemed that bottled beers would dominate over draught beers. Then the development of keg bitters resulted in the wholesale removal of beer engines from pubs and the prospect of the demise of 'real ale'. The past 40 years has seen lager sales outstrip the sale of ales: in 1961, ales and stouts had 99 per cent of the market and lagers 1 per cent; by the 1990s lager had well over 50 per cent of the total beer market.

Currently, cask-conditioned ales are holding market share if sold direct from the cask or though a hand-pull pump. Smooth-flow bitters did well in the late 1990s, initially threatening the cask-conditioned market, but latterly they have grown mainly at the expense of keg bitters. Metered dispense, at least in the south of the country, is in decline. Lagers, both draught and bottled, have seen a shift in appeal from standard strength to premium strength, and cider is following this pattern, with growing sales from a low base.

The landlord's choice

You, as the publican, have to make a decision on the beers you are going to sell guided by the type of pub and the target market discussed in Chapters 3 and 4.

As far as methods of dispense are concerned, you will be governed, at least in part, by the physical restrictions of bar layout and cellar. But you need to look at the dispense systems with which you are operating to see if you can improve them either to your own benefit (ease of working, economy, stock control, cost) or for the benefit of your customers (better beer quality, quicker service, correct temperatures, wider choice).

As much of the equipment is likely to be owned by the brewers, it is often a case of persuading them that changes you recommend are in the interest of higher beer sales – always the most persuasive argument!

Cellar management – the benefits

Although cellar management is not a complex matter, it is one that demands time and care every day of the week as we suggested at the beginning of this chapter.

The benefits of this attention are considerable and have a great influence on the pub's profitability.

Product quality

Beers served in fine condition give your house a reputation for excellence which enhances your professionalism and rubs off on all other activities in the establishment.

Consistency

A cellar and dispense equipment that are immaculately clean and well-organized guarantee that the quality is consistent day in and day out.

Enhanced sales

Beers of consistently high quality encourage existing customers to drink up and have another and bring in new customers to enjoy your products.

Prices

Beers in prime condition can more readily stand that penny or two pence premium.

Wastage

There are five basic rules that must be followed to reduce wastage:

- stock rotation – ensuring no beers go out of date, old or stale;
- correct temperatures – beers always at a temperature acceptable to the customer; no unsaleable beer because of chill haze or over-carbonation;
- clean cellar, beer lines and equipment – no wastage through contamination or fobbing;
- tidiness, organization – beer not lost through spillage, cask disturbance, over-long beer lines;
- good beer-handling practices – particularly with cask-conditioned ales.

The cost of wastage

Let us take the case where a cellar is badly managed and see what losses may occur in a house selling five barrels (180 gallons) a week of draught beer taken as 5 × 18 gallons of cask ale and 5 × 18 gallons of keg beers.

One week's losses:
16 pints cask ale unsaleable (old, out of date)
24 pints cask ale unsaleable (sour, out of date)
12 pints cask ale rejected by customers (too warm, flat)
16 pints lager lost through excessive fobbing at dispense (over carbonation)
8 pints rejected by customers (tainted beer from dirty beer lines)
4 pints lost (badly tapped cask)
24 pints cask ale unsaleable (infected)
84 pints TOTAL

Assuming a wholesale price of 75p a pint (exclusive of VAT), this gives a weekly loss of 84 × 75p = £63 or £3,276 a year.

The loss of 84 pints is 'only' 5.8 per cent of the total draught sales: really bad management could lead to a much higher figure than that.

The professional innkeeper has every reason to be a good cellar manager – it is not only pride at stake but profit as well.

Stock-ordering system

The innkeeper needs to have a method for stock ordering – it is no good waiting until the supplier phones up for an order then guessing at what may be needed.

To hold excessive stock is wasteful, it ties up your capital unnecessarily and perishable goods may well go out of date before sale. Not enough stock and you are letting down your customers and losing a sale.

But how much is enough?

The trade is notoriously fickle and you have to allow for the known fluctuations but after a reasonable time in your inn you will have a fair idea of your pattern of trade.

We will take draught beer ordering as an example but the principles apply to soft drinks or crisps or food for the kitchen or any other regularly ordered items. The steps are as follows:

- calculate your average sale per item per week (or per month if it is a monthly delivery);
- decide on the optimum stock level to give you neither under-stocking nor over-stocking taking into account the 'shelf life' of the items;
- calculate the volume stock you hold on the day the order is placed;
- optimum stock minus current stock is the order to be placed;
- monitor the average sale figure and amend when necessary;
- be flexible for special circumstances.

With beers you will be ordering at least two days ahead of the actual delivery. Remember to allow for this and for the extra twenty-four hours settling time for cask-conditioned ales.

An order book as illustrated in Figure 8.2 is simple and gives information about trade patterns at a glance. Those licensees with personal computers can program such a system into their computers while the most sophisticated electronic tills will calculate stock levels on a running per sale basis.

Wines and spirits

Keeping stocks of wines and spirits is comparatively simple. The main rules are:

- keep spirit stocks as low as practical;
- keep spirits, fortified wines and more expensive wines in a secure, locked cage within your storage area;

Product	Stock (gallons) 2 Jan	Order 2 Jan	Stock 9 Jan	Order 10 Jan	Stock 16 Jan	Order 16 Jan	Stock 23 Jan	Order 23 Jan	Average sales per week (gallons)	Optimum stock level (gallons)
Premium bitter 18 gallons 9 gallons	– 16	– 2 × 9	– 22	– 1 × 9	12	1 × 18 2 × 9			20	30
Standard bitter 18 gallons	25	3 × 18	28	3 × 18	36	2 × 18			50	70
Premium lager 22 gallons 11 gallons	8 11	1 × 22	12 0	1 × 22 1 × 11	15 2	1 × 22 1 × 11			30	40

Standard lager 22 gallons	12	2 × 22	16	2 × 22	10	2 × 22			45	50
Stout 11 gallons	18	–	7	1 × 11	7	1 × 11			10	15
Cider 11 gallons	5	1 × 11	12	–	8	–			5	7
CO_2 cylinder	2	1	1	2	2	1			1.5	3

Figure 8.2 A stock-ordering system. *Notes*: 1. Stock figures are based on dipping part-used ale casks and estimating (by weight) keg beers and cider; 2. An eighteen-gallon keg of premium bitter was ordered on 16th January in anticipation of a sale at a booked birthday party; 3. Sales of cider are below previous average – review product and pricing.

- store vintage wines or wines that you may keep in stock for three months or more on their side, to keep the corks moist and the seal secure.

Soft drinks

Although slightly more expensive, post-mix soft drinks now dominate sales in pubs. The equipment should be kept clean. The syrup used is obviously sticky and regular cleaning is essential.

9 Profit from food

Background

The growth of food sales in pubs and inns has been one of the phenomena of the past thirty years. These sales now represent a significant proportion of the public's spending on food eaten outside the home.

In 1970, it was still exceptional to be offered a decent choice of food in a British pub. In that year, we remember a country inn landlord proudly answering a question on his pub's catering 'Yes, we do food all right – cheese sandwiches on Friday nights'. And he was being serious.

Now it seems that almost every pub in the country offers food and feels compelled to do so. There is a belief among many customers that food in pubs is the easy way for the landlord to make money.

The opposite is more often the truth. We believe more innkeepers have gone out of business or suffered serious financial loss through trying, and failing, to promote a food trade than have ever got into difficulties purely on the drinks side.

The reasons are not hard to see. The pub is set up, and perhaps has been for several hundred years, to sell alcoholic drinks. Dispensing drinks is not technically difficult and does not need equipment expensive to the landlord. Most drinks are delivered in packages of a fixed size (casks, bottles, cans) and sold in prescribed measures. Except for cask ales, drinks have a long shelf life. Deliveries are free, regular and credit is given.

Most products are promoted nationally and/or locally by brewers, distillers or soft drinks manufacturers, often with huge budgets. Innkeepers running free houses are courted by the larger brewers with discounts, loans and special offers.

Compared with selling drinks, the creation of a profitable food operation is usually more difficult and calls for a wide range of skills.

Nevertheless, the decline of the traditional drinks trade and changes in people's social habits have persuaded more and more licensees to turn to food to boost their income. There has, of course, always been a section of the trade that has focused on offering quality food, indeed the very word 'inn' implied that food and refreshment were provided for weary travellers.

But the huge growth in the provision of food in recent years has come, in many cases, from publicans and innkeepers who have had little experience or training in catering. Many have done well, others have suffered serious loss.

Throughout the 1990s in particular, the major brewers, pub retailers and regional brewers have devoted huge sums of money and great effort into building chains of branded food outlets (Beefeater, Miller's Kitchen, Vintage Inns and many more). These are all managed houses and work to a proven formula. They are usually well sited, proficiently run and generate high turnover. They can be a serious threat to the independent licensee's food business.

Don't tackle them head on, work to your strengths: individuality; personal service; personality; flexibility; and choice. Competition can be not only a threat but an opportunity.

Some dos and don'ts

So what are the 'dos and don'ts' of setting up a profitable food operation or indeed in making changes to an existing one?

Define the target market

Do research your market. Where and who are the potential customers? Are there businessmen Monday to Friday lunchtimes?

Couples in the early evening? Older or retired people with money to spend in seeking out an attractive inn? Families for traditional Sunday lunches?

Do consider the opposition. What are they doing that you could do better? What are they **not** offering – is there a gap in the market?

Do decide which segment or segments of the potential market you will target.

Don't try to target every segment – you cannot be all things to all people.

Don't spend money or commit your business in any way until you have made this fundamental decision.

Set your limits

Do understand what you are good at doing.

Don't think you can provide Cordon Bleu catering with nothing behind you but domestic cooking experience.

Do keep the operation as simple as possible.

Don't overstretch yourself or your staff – it is far better to do the basics exceptionally well rather than the sophisticated badly.

Take account of your kitchen

Do understand the limits of your kitchen – its size, facilities, location, capacity.

Do work to your kitchen's strengths and those of your staff.

Don't spend money on kitchen alterations, expensive equipment and staff until you are certain of your food-marketing strategy.

Plan the menu

Do take account of all the dos and don'ts above before deciding on what you will offer and at what times.

Do produce a menu to include dishes which are interesting for your target customers. Remember there was a time when chilli con carne was an unusual and exciting dish to find on an inn's lunchtime menu.

Do have items on your menu which are specialities and for which you wish to become well known, which you do better or with greater originality than anyone else: it may be as simple as the crustiest, tastiest home-made bread, the widest selection of local cheeses or, more ambitiously, the most delicate crème brûlée, the most wonderful boeuf en croute. Whatever it is, you want your customers to talk about it – word of mouth is the very best advertisement for your kitchen.

Don't have a menu that is lacking in choice, your customers need to find dishes that please them not just on one occasion but on repeat visits. But don't make the choice so extensive that the kitchen cannot cope and even the customers are overwhelmed by the endless selection of dishes.

Do plan the menu so that there are items to appeal to the different sections of your target customers. The lunchtime businessmen may want rump steak and all the trimmings but the retired couple at the next table are looking for something much lighter.

Do plan your menu so that the cooking of popular dishes is shared amongst the equipment you have available. You do not want bottlenecks in the kitchen caused by a queue at the grill while the oven stands unused.

Do take account of time. There is no point in a lunchtime menu with dishes that take half an hour to prepare if your customers only have forty minutes for their lunch break.

Do include dishes that allow you to use up leftovers.

Don't allow your menu to become stale and stereotyped.

Get your prices right

Do research what your target customers are prepared to pay and what the opposition is offering. If your prime opposition is doing traditional Sunday lunches, three courses and coffee for £3.95, you will have to be dramatically better to successfully charge £8.95. Maybe this is the moment to produce an untraditional Sunday lunch.

Do decide what GP percentage you are looking for, averaging across the whole food operation and the GP percentage for individual dishes.

Do remember that seasonal foods can vary widely in price from season to out of season. The tomato you slice up on your ploughman's lunch in August may cost you 5p but in February three times as much.

Do cost every dish in detail, not forgetting the couple of sprigs of watercress on the steak, the smear of butter on the bread, the cucumber slices on the salmon.

Do seek a balance of prices across sections of the menu – if every main course is priced at £10.95 you are offering your customers no options to reflect the state of their wallets or their degree of hunger.

Do review your costs and your prices regularly.

Work within your budget

Don't get carried away by the glamour of your new catering project.

Do cost everything carefully, calculate a projected food profit and loss account, and be realistic about forecast takings and overheads.

Don't expect instant success: many experienced people in the trade believe it takes up to 18 months to establish a food business.

Don't spend, or borrow, more than the project can realistically sustain. It is not difficult to commit £30,000 to fitting out a catering kitchen and more on top for creating or refurbishing a dining room or restaurant.

Style of catering

Your style of catering will be governed by:

- the choice of customers or potential customers;
- your and your staff's skills;

- kitchen resources;
- space available for eaters/diners;
- the setting and ambience of the pub or inn;
- your financial resources.

Taking due account of these restrictions or opportunities, you will establish your catering at the appropriate level which could be anything from bar snacks Monday to Saturday lunchtimes to full à la carte restaurant fourteen sessions a week.

Each strategy can be equally valid if it best meets the demands of the inn's particular circumstances.

Most financial disasters occur because the innkeeper sets out to provide catering which does not match the profile of his or her customers or which is beyond his or her capabilities. If the customers want simple, value-for-money, filling meals, it is pointless to offer nouvelle cuisine, however exquisitely presented. If the customers are more sophisticated and are seeking an experience, not just filling up with calories, you will offend them if you pile the plate high with chips.

There was a time some years ago when pub catering was simpler so that what the kitchen could produce was what the customer was offered. Now, with the huge growth of the catering market, there has been the corresponding growth of the catering supplier, not just of raw materials but of prepared dishes.

It is this factor, together with freezers and microwaves, which has changed the face of catering in Britain. It is now possible for unskilled caterers to put before their customers a range of dishes which their own unaided efforts could not produce and which their kitchens could certainly not cope with.

The dos and don'ts listed earlier are therefore influenced by the degree to which prepared dishes, vegetables and sweets are included in the menu.

Some of the pros and cons of using bought-in prepared dishes are:

For:

- reliability of source;
- consistency of product;
- ease of preparation;
- no skilled labour needed;

- portion control;
- little preparation time;
- speed from storage to serving;
- reduced wastage.

Against:
- loss of caterer's individuality;
- a degree of blandness;
- same dishes available in competitive establishments;
- higher initial price;
- specific storage requirements.

The decision you make about using bought-in dishes or creating your own will, in the end, be judged by your customers and how they perceive the quality and variety of food you are offering.

But catering is not just about the dishes on the menu: often it is the apparently smaller matters that undermine the inexperienced or over-ambitious innkeeper's efforts. The inn that aspires to a quality reputation for food will quickly get a negative reaction from its customers if the black pepper is not in a pepper mill, the vinaigrette is not home-made, mustard is in a tube. However deep the carpet and leatherbound the menu, the customer will resent the shortcuts the innkeeper is taking and become suspicious of everything on the menu.

There are worse horrors that even the general local uses at its peril: brown sauce in plastic packets, tomato sauce in plastic tomatoes, vinegar in glass bottles to spread its pervasive smell around neighbouring tables, plastic cutlery, artificial flowers in twee glass vases on dining tables.

A quality food-led inn does not depend upon lavish surroundings, waiters in bow ties and expensive menus. Quality is established by a much subtler blend of food, service and ambience in which everything combines to satisfy the customer's expectations.

Some of the most memorable and popular establishments today have stone-flagged floors, blackboard menus, the diners eat at scrubbed tables, service is informal but efficient and the food is original, not cheap but value for money. Such places are typically owner-run or owner/chef-run and bring a welcome breath of fresh air to the British inn scene.

Kitchen layouts

Very few innkeepers have the luxury of a perfect kitchen layout. Because so many inns are old and have been through various structural changes over the years, the catering kitchen is often a relatively recent conversion. Kitchens are frequently small, awkwardly shaped and inconvenient. Nevertheless, there are numerous inns up and down the land which produce an astonishing variety and quantity of food from kitchens which have all these negative attributes.

The important elements are planning, layout and equipment.

Planning

- Menu – planning in relation to the kitchen's capabilities has already been emphasized.
- Staff – planning to have the right number and quality of staff available when they are most valuable to you.
- Food – planning for the raw materials and prepared foods to be readily to hand.

Layout

A catering kitchen, whether for producing simple cold dishes or elaborate gourmet food, needs to be logically laid out. Ideally, there is a natural flow from preparation area to cooking to plating and serving. There should be the minimum opportunity for staff carrying out different functions getting in each other's way. Dirty dishes and wash-up should be as far as possible separate from the main cooking area and as convenient as possible for waiting staff to reach.

If you need help in planning the layout of your kitchen, there are many specialist firms of catering kitchen designers.

We look at three sample kitchen layouts in Figures 9.1–9.3 later in the chapter.

Equipment

There is a huge choice of catering equipment available, large and small items, the relatively inexpensive to the vastly expensive. Choose carefully, look at different suppliers' ranges, compare prices but above all else look for fitness for purpose. Get the oven or grill or toaster or microwave that best matches your needs. The equipment should cope comfortably with your periods of greatest pressure, not be struggling to meet your demands of it. Such a struggle only leads to delay and frustration in the kitchen and over-stressing the equipment causing expensive repair and maintenance bills. That extra cubic foot in the refrigerator, the room for an additional two steaks under the grill, the extractor system that really works are invaluable assets that can make the difference between efficiency and making do.

Cost is, of course, a key factor. If you are on a tight budget, it is worth considering the choice of second-hand catering equipment. There are a number of reputable companies that deal in such items and the savings can be considerable.

Washing up

There will always be the need for deep-sink facilities for washing up large pots, pans and special items. But the dishwasher has increasingly become a vital item of catering equipment. That it should get the dishes clean is clearly a basic requirement but you also need to choose the best machine in terms of speed of washing cycle and quickness of drying after removal from the dishwasher without the need for drying with a cloth.

Storage and deliveries

Space and equipment for storage of food is almost as important as cooking space and is often overlooked by the inexperienced. You will need storage space for:

- dry goods;
- fresh fruit and vegetables;
- meats;
- fish;
- chilled food;
- frozen food;

each requiring different conditions and temperatures. The more storage space you have with food well laid out and organized, the better your management of food stocks and the less risk of wastage or food deterioration.

Storage space or the lack of it is a major factor when organizing your deliveries or collection of foodstuffs. If you rely largely on a weekly delivery of frozen foods, your storage needs will be very different and more expensive than if you have a largely fresh food menu with deliveries of meat, fish and vegetables several times a week.

Environmental health officers (EHOs)

We have already suggested that most innkeepers will not enjoy the luxury of designing and fitting out a brand new kitchen but will have to work with something less than the ideal. It is particularly important in these circumstances that the highest standards of health, hygiene and safety are practised.

The responsibility for seeing that such standards are maintained lies with the EHOs. These men and women have achieved something of an unenviable reputation as the terrors of the catering trade.

The innkeeper needs to understand that EHOs are people whom he or she has to work with, not against. They cannot be ignored, threatened or bullied. Their authority stretches to all food serving, food-handling or food-storage areas of the inn; in this context drink is food so the cellar is as critical as the kitchen.

EHOs have the power to close down an establishment that is a danger to public health or to issue statutory notices ordering remedial work to be carried out within a stipulated time, typically fourteen or twenty-eight days.

The golden rules for innkeepers are:

- co-operate with the EHO on an initial visit;
- listen to points he or she makes and explain your position and the difficulties you may have;
- do not lose your temper;
- accept valid criticisms with good grace;
- volunteer to put simple things right straightaway;
- bargain for time to correct more fundamental faults;
- understand the difference between those items that the EHO can enforce legally and those actions that he or she is requesting: be prepared to negotiate – many aspects of the legislation are open to different interpretations.

The commonest faults the EHOs have to take action against, in addition to straightforward shortcomings in basic cleanliness, are

- cracked or broken floor coverings;
- work surfaces that are chipped or scratched;
- walls and ceilings not having sound, impermeable, readily cleansable surfaces;
- faulty or dangerous equipment;
- food stored incorrectly or at the wrong temperature;
- insects or vermin in a food area;
- inadequate washing or washing up facilities;
- dangerous working environment for staff.

Set yourself the highest standards; by so doing you will be avoiding most of the problems before they arise.

It is not just a matter of law, it is in the best interests of the professional innkeeper to be recognized as having exemplary standards of health, hygiene and safety throughout his or her food and drink operation.

Recent years have seen several high-profile health scares, some serious, other perhaps over-dramatized. The incidence of reported food poisoning has certainly grown, with the outcome that the press, politicians and public have all become much more aware of the dangers of bad food-handling practices. The setting up by the government of the Food Standards Agency is the most obvious result.

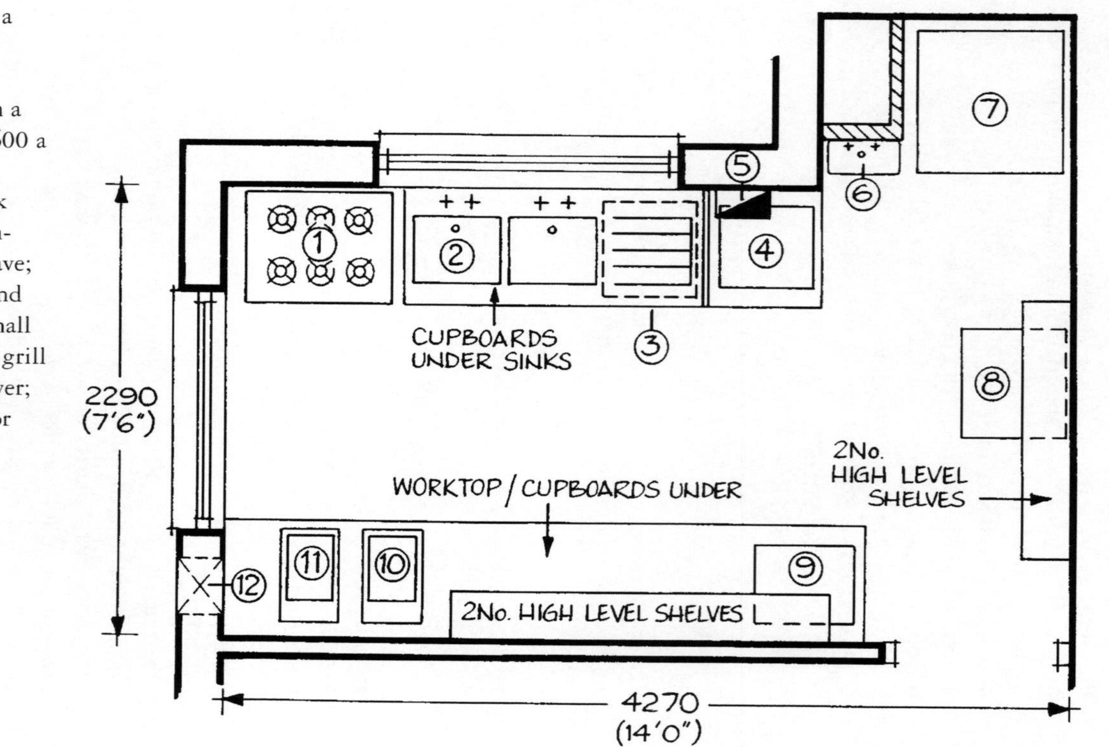

Figure 9.1 A kitchen in a good-quality general local producing food on six lunchtimes each week with a food turnover of around £600 a week. *Key*: 1, compact six-burner oven; 2, double sink with single drainer; 3, dish-washer (under); 4, microwave; 5, insectecutor; 6, wash hand basin; 7, large fridge; 8, small freezer; 9, microwave with grill on top; 10, freestanding fryer; 11, inset fryer; 12, extractor fan.

Innkeepers, therefore, are ever-increasingly in the spotlight, particularly with their catering operations. You must make sure that you do everything right; if you neglect food safety you not only endanger your customers, you also put your business in peril, or in extreme cases risk a potential prison sentence.

Some food operations

We first visited an owner-run free house on a main road through a large village: one-bar general local; food served Monday to Saturday only, lunchtimes 12 till 2 pm.

The catering kitchen also has to serve as a domestic kitchen (Figure 9.1).

Joint owner, June, organizes the kitchen, buys, plans menus and prepares all those dishes made on the premises. She employs a young woman to actually run the lunchtime kitchen and has trained her as cook.

June: 'Our policy is to give real value for money food. It's what makes our lunchtimes really work. We are nicely busy most days with the majority regular customers, women and men, although we also get people stopping who are driving through'.

The menu is uncomplicated: good choice of sandwiches and toasted sandwiches (£1.30 to £2); burgers and ploughman's, soup, salads (£3.25 to £4.50), omelettes with fries and vegetables or salad (£2.75 to £3.95) and seven main dishes, e.g. 6 oz sirloin with fries, vegetables and trimmings £5.75; gammon ham with egg, fries and baked beans or vegetables £3.50; chicken goujons with barbecue or sweet and sour dip, fries and vegetables £3.90. The most expensive dish is fillet steak (6 oz) at £8.75.

June: 'I also put on two 'specials' each day – two of the most popular would be home-made steak and kidney pie or liver and onions both served with potatoes and two vegetables'.

Sweets at £1.95, cheese and biscuits and coffee complete the food offering.

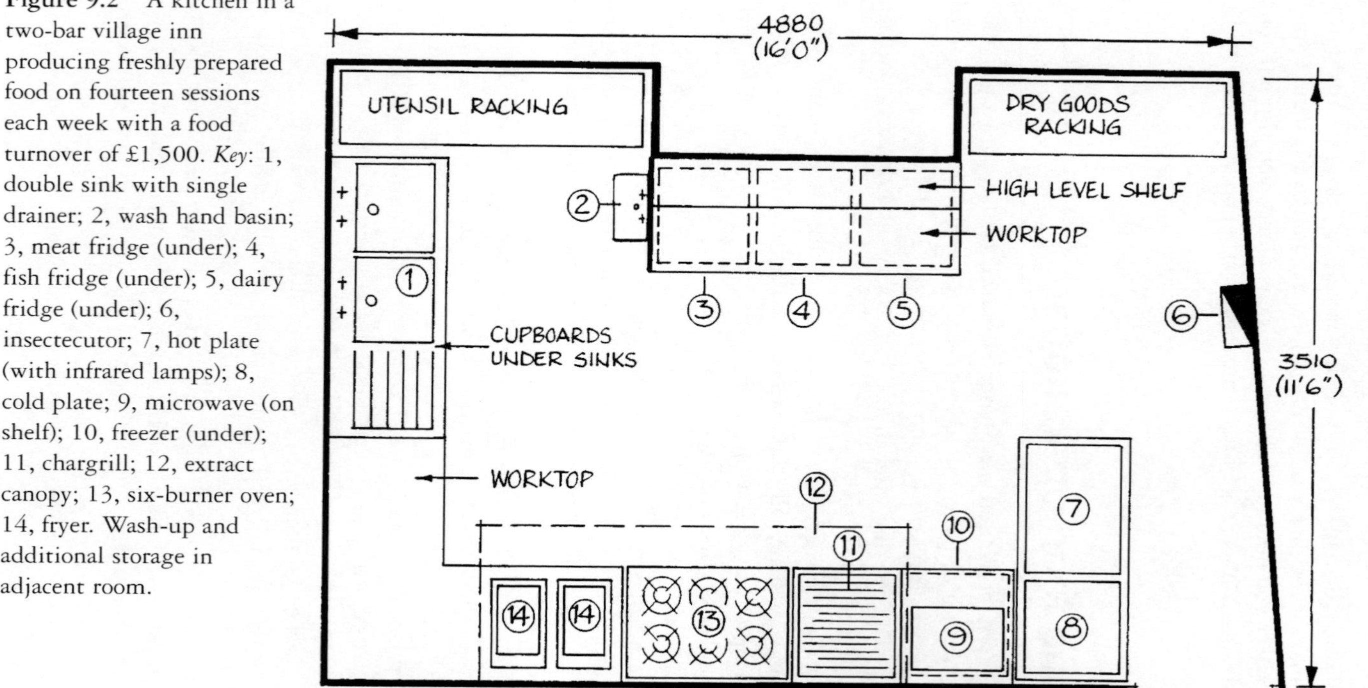

Figure 9.2 A kitchen in a two-bar village inn producing freshly prepared food on fourteen sessions each week with a food turnover of £1,500. *Key*: 1, double sink with single drainer; 2, wash hand basin; 3, meat fridge (under); 4, fish fridge (under); 5, dairy fridge (under); 6, insectecutor; 7, hot plate (with infrared lamps); 8, cold plate; 9, microwave (on shelf); 10, freezer (under); 11, chargrill; 12, extract canopy; 13, six-burner oven; 14, fryer. Wash-up and additional storage in adjacent room.

June: 'Our customers are happy with our prices and the generous portions. The menu is about right now. We experimented with Sunday lunch but families choose to go out to the country pubs more. For the same reason, we tend to do better on food in the winter than in the summer because we have no garden'.

'We buy in our steaks and fish pre-packed but I make all our 'specials', prepare them in advance for the cook'.

The kitchen is small but works well for the chosen menu. The compact gas six-burner oven is invaluable and the two fryers are kept busy. June: 'Nearly everyone in this pub wants chips'.

She values her large commercial refrigerator and would like a bigger commercial microwave. The dishwasher is domestic size.

Food turnover averages £600 per week.

Our next visit was to a tenanted two-bar traditional inn in a medium-sized village: lounge bar devoted mainly to diners, twenty-eight covers; customers overspill into saloon bar at busy times; meals fourteen sessions a week.

The kitchen (Figure 9.2) is designed to be run by one person, normally the tenant, Peter. He has trained up a young man to a standard where he can run the kitchen on Peter's day off or assist at exceptionally busy times.

The menu is designed to the kitchen's strengths with five starters or snacks at £2.50, six lower-priced main courses (e.g. grilled brochette of kidney, liver and bacon served on rice with a mild mustard sauce £5); five medium-priced courses (e.g. escalope of pork baked with apple, sultanas and cider served with a choice of potatoes and salad or fresh vegetables £7.50) and four more expensive courses (e.g. 10 oz fillet steak plain grilled or with a cream and green peppercorn sauce with choice of potatoes and salad or vegetables £10).

Filled jacket potatoes and ploughman's are also offered plus a choice of sweets and coffee.

Meat, fish and vegetables are all fresh with dishes prepared in the kitchen. Sauces are made in advance. Sweets are frozen. Peter: 'I get excellent service from my local suppliers and competitive prices. With little frozen food bought, I save considerably on storage costs'.

The six-burner oven is the vital piece of equipment. 'I couldn't exist without it' says Peter. The grill also has its valued part to play but the menu and custom are such that the deep fryer and microwave are the least used items.

Peter: 'Because of the style of catering we offer, customers' waiting time for a main course would average twenty to thirty minutes from ordering but this is wholly acceptable and indeed reinforces the freshly prepared image'.

Food is fetched from the kitchen by waiting staff. Wash up is organized separately. Peter: 'One of my best buys was the commercial dishwasher, not cheap but very quick and efficient'.

Food turnover is around £1,500 a week but the kitchen could cope with up to £3,000.

Our final destination was an inn and restaurant tucked away in a village on the edge of a busy market town; a high-quality pub restaurant but where bar food and bar drinks are also very important. Customers come from a wide area and appreciate the attractive stoned-flagged bar on two levels opening into a fifty cover beamed restaurant that can, if necessary, be increased with additional covers if the occasion demands it.

We were interested in this particular inn because it illustrated the way in which an experienced caterer set about developing a quality business. Christian and Carol took over the lease in 1990. 'It suited me at the time' says Christian 'to take a leasehold property rather than a freehold; that way I limited my investment and risk, did not have the pressure of large borrowings but could develop the trade in exactly the way I wanted'. In 1998 they sold-on their lease but the lessons from their tenure are relevant to our readers. Their successors continue to run the business on similar lines.

Extensive bar menu from 12 till 2 pm including typically sixteen main items from £4.50 to £5.50: some favourites are home-made chicken and ham pie £4.50; Japanese king prawns and garlic dip £5.25; crêpes with choice of fillings and granary bread £4.50. Up to ten salads are on offer (from £3.95 to £6.50) plus filled baps, ploughman's (£2.95 to £3.25), pâté and a large selection of home-made sweets. The menu changes daily and, with the exception of peas and leaf spinach, no frozen vegetables are bought in.

In addition to filtered coffee, espresso and cappuccino are offered. 'The espresso machine was a marvellous investment' says Christian 'with grinder you are talking about £4,000 but marvellous coffee and no waste'.

There is a fixed-price lunchtime menu in the restaurant (£11.75 for three courses and coffee, £13.75 on Sundays) and an evening set menu at £15.95. The à la carte menu lunchtime and evenings is extensive without being overwhelming: sixteen starters (e.g. moules à la marinière £5.25; warm salad of pigeon and hazelnuts £4.25; prawns and chutney curry £3.75); fifteen main courses (e.g. coulibiac of fresh Scotch salmon £8.50; magret of duck with lime and ginger £9.25; fillet of pork forestière £8.75). Selection of fresh vegetables £2.95. In addition, there are up to six daily specials and a selection of fresh fish and shellfish (e.g. sea bass, red mullet, lobster, Dover sole). The fresh fish is delivered three times a week. The selection from the sweet trolley is £2.95 and cheeses £3.50. Around 80 per cent of the sweets are freshly made in house.

The aim is quality of raw materials all the time and to be always looking for new ideas in creating dishes. Very little is bought in except for items like scampi so this is a very labour-intensive operation, particularly in the kitchen where the average number of staff would be six. The monthly wage bill for the whole inn is over £10,000 each month.

The basic layout of the kitchen and much of the equipment were inherited by Christian when he took over the inn. The changes made give us the kitchen layout shown in Figure 9.3. He also had built, to his design, the walk-in cold store, costing around £5,000, and could not have managed without it. It is used for fresh vegetables, cooked meats and, for short periods, fresh meat and fish as well.

Like many businesses of this size, it was a family concern and Carol's sister had responsibility for producing all the bar food orders. Her record was 140 dishes in one day! The restaurant is handled by the four chefs. Although there is a clear 'pecking

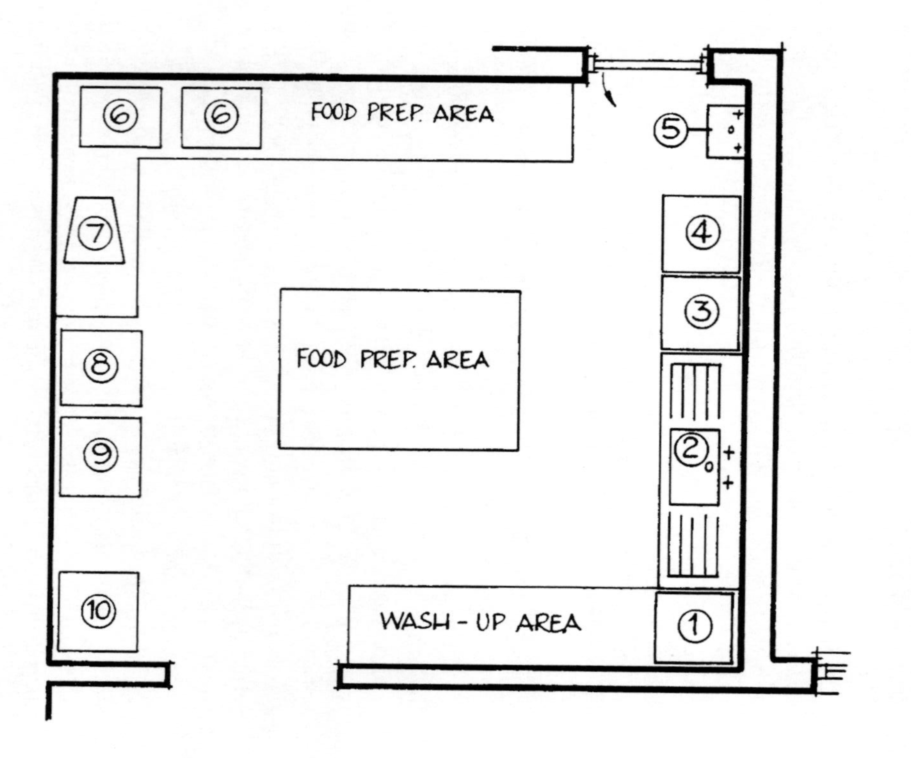

Figure 9.3 A kitchen in a high-quality restaurant and inn producing both à la carte and bar meals with food turnover in excess of £5,000 per week. *Key*: 1, pass-through dishwasher; 2, single sink with double drainer; 3, ice maker; 4, kitchen wine fridge; 5, wash hand basin; 6, microwave; 7, slicer; 8, freezer; 9, fridge; 10, sweet fridge; 11, wine fridge; 12, double fryer; 13, Mealsteam (under); 14, six-burner oven; 15, extract canopy; 16, double wash-up sink; 17, large meat fridge; 18, fish grill; 19, hot plate; 20, bain marie (mobile). There are in addition a purpose-built walk-in cold-room, a walk-in dry-goods store and two large deep freezers located near the kitchen.

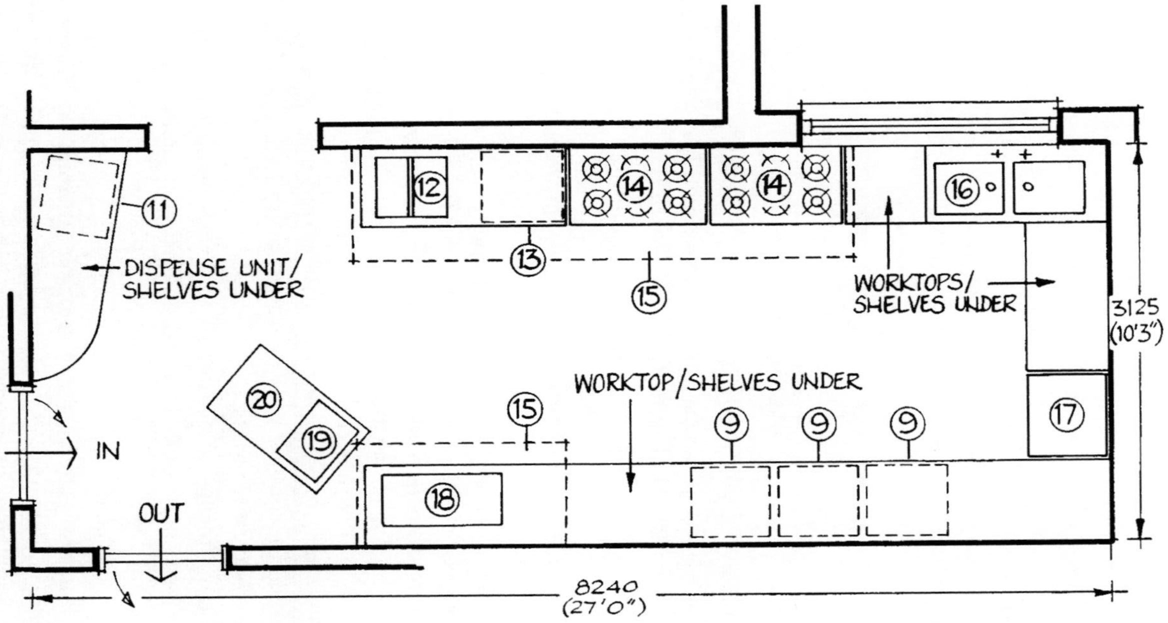

Figure 9.3 *(continued)*

order', they have to work as a team, often under tremendous pressure.

The main cooking area is not ideally laid out. 'Had it been possible' says Christian 'I would have knocked out the dividing wall and replanned the kitchen totally so that the wash up and prep were nearest the dining area with the main cooking area beyond. As it is, the waiters have to cross the cooking area with dirty dishes and bar food orders. But I had to work with what was there, the world is not perfect'. Most of the equipment, however, is designed to the needs of the restaurant although he considered swapping the Mealsteam (which he rarely used) for a small steamer. The two gas six-burner stoves are side by side and get heavy usage. The main refrigerators are product-specific, increasingly important with the tougher hygiene regulations on temperature control. The total kitchen equipment would cost over £50,000 to replace and therefore has to work very hard for its keep.

The quality of staff is clearly important in this type of operation. Christian and Carol chose their staff carefully but were in the strong position of having the skills, knowledge and experience to run the kitchen and restaurant themselves. There is no room for the amateur in this scale of operation.

'One of the keys to success is getting the menus right, firstly to attract restaurant customers but also to keep the balance right with the bar food trade which is important. The bar menu must complement the restaurant menu, not fight with it. The skill of the chef is to plan his menus so that nothing is wasted. For instance, if yesterday there had been more red peppers than, in the end, had been needed for a restaurant main course dish, then today, on the bar menu would be a cold mousse of red peppers and tomato sauce. I hate waste in the kitchen it can so quickly erode gross profits.'

Christian's menus changed daily and were produced on the in-house wordprocessor. 'It saved an awful lot of money on printing and, because we used special-quality paper, the menus looked professional too'.

One final tip from Christian came on ordering. He always places large orders for non-perishable goods, wine for instance, at the beginning of the month so as to allow maximum credit but also gets the maximum discounts for the quantity delivered. Most of the goods are therefore sold before they need to be paid for. A good tip for any business!

10 The downside

What have grockles, emmetts and roses around the door in common? Not a great deal really, except they are all disparaging terms, the first being the description of holidaymakers by the indigenous populations of Devon and Cornwall and the last one commonly used to describe applicants who have unrealistic and naive expectations of how pleasant it would be to run a pub or inn. When tourists are scarce, it is with wistful nostalgia that the west country innkeeper refers to grockles. In similar fashion, the turbulent times that the licensed trade has endured have largely dispelled the myth of 'roses around the door'.

In this chapter, we cover the downside of the business:

- drunkenness and alcohol abuse;
- drug abuse;
- violence;
- under-age drinking;
- handling complaints;
- drinking and driving.

We also discuss the need for door control in certain types of pubs, relationships with the police, avoiding causing a nuisance to neighbours, difficulties at closing time, bad language and how to avoid violent or difficult situations arising.

Well over half the nation now thoroughly disapproves of smoking and the tobacco industry, with the percentage growing. Smoking is banned in many public places, offices, theatres and, of course, an increasing number of restaurants and even bars. The public's attitude to smoking and the tobacco industry 20 years ago was concerned, questioning but very much more tolerant. The public's disposition then reminds us of their attitude now to alcohol and the pub industry. So what will be the attitude to alcohol in five, ten or twenty years' time? Will it go the same way as tobacco? Will there be a reduction to zero in the alcohol to blood count before driving? Will the anti-alcohol lobby win the propaganda war linking alcohol to all the nation's woes?

If the answer to these questions were to be a qualified and gradual yes, then this would inevitably mean that business in the licensed trade would at best be static but most likely continue to decline.

When business is growing steadily with no real pressure on profits and the survival of your business is not under threat, it is much simpler to address and conform to the rules. With business in decline and your livelihood threatened, it is all too easy to succumb to the pressures to serve after hours, to serve a good customer a further drink knowing he or she has had too much already or to accept custom from free spenders whose language and behaviour you would not otherwise tolerate.

But all sections of the trade have a long-term interest in presenting to the nation the most positive, favourable and socially concerned attitudes towards alcohol and the way it is handled by licensees and customers alike. The British pub, when properly run, is a social asset of the greatest value and adds immeasurably to the well-being of people in all walks of life.

The trade neglects its current and future image at its peril.

Drink driving and drunken behaviour

As a licensee, it is your clear responsibility to ensure that you run an orderly house. Although you will be getting a large proportion of your income from sales of alcoholic drinks, you must not allow drunkenness on the premises nor knowingly serve someone with alcohol when you believe he or she is already intoxicated. You may perhaps consider you have some moral responsibility for the conduct of your customers once they have left you. If this is the case, then it does not need the law to curb the amount of alcohol that you serve to an individual.

You need to strike a balance. One very good and experienced innkeeper said to us recently 'I don't like other people's second-hand alcohol in my pub'. He was very happy for people to have a good evening in his pub, would even drive them home if it were necessary, but he was not prepared to serve people who had done most of their drinking elsewhere and finished up with him later in the evening causing problems and disruption. It is a simple but important message:

- refuse service to those entering your premises who appear to you to have had enough alcohol already.

Another excellent innkeeper of our acquaintance has an attractive and busy inn about two miles outside a large town. His trade from 9 pm onwards is young but good quality. He has negotiated special rates with a local taxi firm to get his customers back into town. All the customer has to do is to ask at the bar for a taxi and a small fleet will start to ferry customers back into town at closing time. No illegal drinking and driving, no problem clearing the pub at closing time and very well-satisfied and therefore loyal customers. The moral is:

- get organized in advance and you can avoid most of the problems that come at closing time.

Another licensee of a traditional food-led inn, five miles out of a large town, never drinks alcohol throughout the evening as he has purchased a minibus and ferries his customers back into town and sometimes to their homes. Most customers will have dined with him and he makes a nominal charge for this service on their bills, enough incidentally to pay for the running of the vehicle. His sales of wines, brandies and liqueurs are well above average because his customers relax in the knowledge of a trouble-free journey home. So:

- when planning your business and capital expenditure, give thought to how your customers will get home.

Another popular way of handling the problem of customers getting home is to encourage the 'nominated driver'. It has to be the way forward for one volunteer to stay clear of alcohol and drive his group home. It is a responsible act to encourage this by supplying a full range of interesting alcohol-free or low alcohol products and perhaps give some price or other incentive to the nominated driver in a party of four or five.

- It is good practice to overtly promote a safe drinking and driving policy.

Although drunkenness can occur in any pub or inn, it tends to be more of a problem in town centres and to be associated with youth and often accompanied by violence. It is difficult to think of any town or city on a Friday or Saturday evening that does not have groups of young men and women moving from pub to pub and on to a club from 9 pm onwards.

There is no substitute for experience when trading in this environment. It is essential to remain alert and to anticipate trouble before it starts. It is likely that you will set ground rules so that your staff will react in a predictable way when problems arise. Some of the more obvious rules you might have:

- Only allow customers into your bar in small manageable numbers.
- Try to get a higher than average ratio of young women to young men. Keep the numbers manageable.
- Have sufficient, well-trained and efficient bar staff so that waiting for service is not a problem.
- Make sure customers are acknowledged quickly and served in rotation. Tempers flare when customers are served out of turn.
- Avoid over-crowding. Try to encourage customers away from the bar service area into seated areas. Fights often occur when people jostle each other and drinks are spilt. Young men have been known to lose all control when a drink is spilt down their new silk tie.

- Avoid serving drinks like 'snakebite', a mix of cider and lager, and especially watch out for the 'super' version made with super-strength lager and cider.
- Clear glasses and empty ashtrays regularly. Too many glasses around could make a small scuffle into a bloody incident.
- Give good value in everything that you do, be it drink or food prices or entertainment. You want your customers on your side and not feeling antagonistic.
- Be firm, be fair but be friendly. Set your standards and make sure all your customers know them. Avoid being hard one day and much softer the next. Most customers, and particularly young people, react much better to pubs where the ground rules are known and consistently implemented.
- You have the ultimate sanction of barring customers who misbehave. Use it sparingly but consistently and take care not to relent too easily. It is no use barring someone if he knows he will be allowed back in a couple of days' time.
- Stay sober. You must anticipate trouble before it starts and you must deal with it skilfully, with as little risk to you, your staff and your customers as possible.
- Always try to talk a difficult customer out of your pub. Only resort to force if absolutely necessary. Do not bar him or her that evening but remember who it is and bar them when they next come in sober and more sensible.
- Watch out for customers smuggling flasks of spirits into your bar and adding it to drinks bought. Apart from lost profits, this can have a disproportionate effect on drunkenness because of freely poured spirits.
- Have sufficient staff to allow you to move around the customers and build up a friendly rapport with them. You will appreciate having most of your customers on your side if you do ever get trouble.

Although these rules are especially important in town centres or where trade is young, they also apply to all pubs. The greater the risk of drink-related violence, the more alert you must be. It is a sad fact that many seemingly mature men in their thirties and forties can become totally anti-social when drunk so it is certainly not just the young who can cause trouble.

Door control

In town and city centres, many of the bar doors will be manned by doormen, some of whom will be poorly trained and selected for their brawn rather than their brain. Although there is some evidence of better training for doormen to help them in their role to keep trouble out of the pub, impose a dress code and handle trouble as it arises, often in reality, they act as a challenge to youths who, having had a lager or two, feel they have to prove their courage to their peer group. Any individual running a town centre pub should try very hard to avoid taking on doormen and, if necessary, take on the role himself or herself. It cannot be good policy to allow doormen to make your customer selection for you. The tendency is to finish up with inadequate criteria such as 'no trainers' or 'designer jeans only' or 'over 25s only'. There is a need for much more meaningful customer selection measures and the person likely to understand these best will be the licensee.

With all the drawbacks of doormen, some town centre licensees would not feel able to control their pubs without this kind of back-up. Some reach a compromise by having one or two doormen inside the bar rather than on the door. Their role is to snuff out trouble before it really gets started.

The police in some areas are concerned about not only the doormen but the companies who supply them to the pubs. There are dark hints of protection rackets and competing doormen-supplying companies making trouble for each other.

- So, even if you are getting some problems in your pub, do think twice before you resort to taking on door control.

Problems in the estate local

Some estate locals are very difficult to run with the licensee having to cope with the full range of anti-social behaviour from drugs to drunkenness, from vandalism to violence and often an unpleasant cocktail made up of each of these ingredients with a dash of threatening behaviour added for good measure.

Few people have the particular talents needed to trade in this environment but, if you have and can keep the pub consistently trouble-free, then there are good profits to be made. You do not need to be a sixteen-stone 'bruiser' or even a particularly hard person. You need to understand the people you are serving, to like and respect them as individuals, to be able to command their respect and have the reputation for standing no nonsense nor putting up with any bad behaviour. This needs a certain type of personal courage to enable you to stand up to the small number of troublemakers. Once you get the ringleaders into line, then the others will follow. This will then allow you to stamp your personality on the pub at an early stage. The objective is to get the vast majority of customers on your side, giving them a pride in 'their' pub and, from then on, working with you to keep it safe and secure.

It is rare that this transformation of a difficult pub is done by physical strength. Often, it is quite small men and even women who do the job best, perhaps because their lack of physical stature means they do not present a challenge to the more aggressive customers. If you speak to licensees who are successfully running this style of pub, you will find that they have a strong sense of community, they are very proud of what they are achieving and they feel they play a prominent role in the community that they live and work in.

It is sometimes necessary to bar customers from this type of pub but this must be done thoughtfully. By barring one person too hastily, you could alienate a whole family. Make sure you learn family relationships early so that, if you do have to bar a member of it, you will at least know the maximum number of customers you are likely to lose.

Some years ago, a couple running a not notably difficult pub started barring young men for bad language. They did it without first deciding their objectives and finished up with an empty pub. The local lads decided being barred from this pub was good for their street credibility and it became a sport with youngsters vying with each other to get themselves barred. Needless to say, the couple concerned lost most of their turnover and left the trade in despair six months after they had joined it.

Under-age drinking

The problem of under-age drinking is a major one. There is little doubt that some unscrupulous licensees quite deliberately take a chance and knowingly serve young people. The penalties can, and should, be severe for these licensees. The law is clear on this subject, which we cover in the next chapter, but there are a few anomalies which even experienced licensees may find surprising.

For the average innkeeper, trying to operate the business in a responsible way, the under-age problem is far from straightforward. How do you tell a seventeen-year-old from an eighteen-year-old? If you ask their age and it subsequently turns out that they were less than eighteen, you may still be liable. You asked because you had doubts and, because you had doubts, you should not have served him or her. All sorts of initiatives have been tried including proof-of-age identity cards but none has yet been a total success. The sign 'over twenty-ones only' or even 'over twenty-fives only' is an attempt to avoid under-age customers.

Bad language

Bad language will always feature in some pubs and the best that a licensee can do is to keep it within bounds. Language that would be totally unacceptable in a traditional inn could, in some circumstances, be tolerated in some other types of pub. Bad language directed in a hostile way against a licensee, staff or fellow customer is never acceptable but, if it is being spoken in normal conversation and is not offending anyone else, then there is little that can or perhaps should be done about it.

Drug abuse

You hear commentators on current affairs linking drug and alcohol abuse. This, in a way, is part of the anti-alcohol lobby but sadly they are able to make some connections. With the comparative high price of lager and the low price of cannabis a mixture of the two is all too common. This gives innkeepers a real problem, as a customer, after smoking a joint or two, just drinks a couple of pints and quickly goes from being no problem to causing havoc. Very difficult to detect and the change in mood almost instant but a major problem for the licensee.

Drug taking and drug pushing are easier to detect and usually only go on in poorly supervised pubs. The pub toilets are the favoured place for these activities but in some cases they go on in full, but unseeing, view of the innkeeper and staff. There is little worse than getting a reputation as a drugs pub and if you have any suspicion that it is happening then consult the police without delay. They not only offer advice and training on drugs detection but also help you tackle the problem. Their stance will be much more hostile if you are allowing drug taking and pushing without attempting to do anything about it. So speak to the police, in confidence, at the first sign of trouble.

There are so many drugs that are now regularly abused it needs a specialist to put them into context. Police, in most areas, run training schemes where you will be taught to recognize the look and the smell of the various drugs and the symptoms they produce in their users. You will find it an invaluable use of half a day.

Alcohol abuse

Alcohol abuse is sometimes more difficult to recognize. It is easy to spot groups of people sitting around on park benches with bottles of British fortified wine or strong cider. These rarely use pubs as they prefer to get their supplies a little cheaper and amazingly some shops seem willing to oblige.

Others, often quite smart, middle-aged alcoholics, also tend to purchase their alcohol at wholesale prices. You do find them in pubs but they often hold their liquor well and cause few problems.

The more serious problem for pubs is the younger drinker, sometimes egged on by his or her mates, who will drink excessively and dangerously. A combination of strong lager, spirits and inexperience can be a lethal combination. A good licensee keeps this kind of drinking in tight check.

It is an innkeeper's legal and moral responsibility to control drunkenness. The good news is that if you do this well it will benefit your business and increase your turnover in the long term.

The Portman Group is an organization set up and funded by the major brewers to help the industry compete in the war of words with the anti-alcohol lobby. They project an attitude of responsibility and moderation and in the main their values should also be yours.

Relationship with the police

Many innkeepers' only contact with the police will be a cup of coffee or an off-duty drink with their local bobby – friendly, supportive and serving the community in their different ways – a bit of advice on security or maybe an occasional word about drinking-up time. In the situations we have been describing in this chapter, the role of the police is often much higher profile.

The police are usually supportive of licensees doing a good job in difficult circumstances but critical of those who are not able to keep control of their pubs. A licensee who has regularly to call the police for help to regain order will soon be seen as unsuitable. If that same licensee lets the events in his or her pub take their course without calling for assistance, he or she will quickly get a reputation for not being capable of control.

If you are contemplating taking on a pub with a bad reputation speak to the local police before accepting the job. If you agree with them an action plan to clean up the business, they in turn will support you and give you assistance with your difficult task. The clear moral is:

- Make early contact with the police, listen to their advice and work with them, not against them.

Getting on with your neighbours

With the changes in the licensing laws that allow an objection to your licence at any full licensing session, it is even more essential that you get on with your neighbours. Too much noise, late-night car doors slamming, bad parking, vandalism or just being too busy for the size of the pub can all give rise to problems with neighbours. The general public is gradually starting to understand the powers they now have regarding objections to a licence. The Licensing Magistrates nearly always listen to the complaints of neighbours, especially if they are well organized or have grouped together. The result can be a closed pub or restrictions on the licence that make future trading not worthwhile

Do not wait for trouble but anticipate it. Meet your neighbours, ask them about problems the pub may be causing them and do something about it. Apart from this being good business practice, it is also just good manners.

Handling complaints

Anticipating problems and addressing them before they get too serious is the underlying theme throughout this chapter. Top innkeepers anticipate complaints and deal with them often before they have been voiced. Things go wrong in the best ordered businesses and, the busier you are, the more chance there is of things starting to go askew. If food is delayed or a problem is developing, do not wait for the customer to complain but get in to apologize, give an explanation and outline your plan on how you are getting back on track. A drink on the house, given in time, can often turn a problem into a positive benefit. If a group of four has to wait for their meal much longer than is reasonable, a bottle of wine delivered with an apology for the delay could ensure that you see them again on a future occasion. It has always surprised us that a bottle of wine costing no more than £2.50, given before an actual complaint has been made, can impress and please even the most cynical customer. The first golden rule is:

- anticipate the complaint and deal with it in an apparently generous way.

It never pays to argue with any customer who is complaining about the quality of a product. Your opinion that the product is perfectly acceptable is completely irrelevant to the complainant who equally clearly thinks it is not acceptable. So replace the pint of beer, the glass of wine or a meal with an apology and with a smile. You will find that, at the end of the year, the actual cost of replacements is extremely small but that your reputation will have improved as a result. If you are unlucky enough to have a regular complainer and the complaints are not justified, then perhaps you just replace his drink or meal one more time and suggest politely to him that it may be better if he found somewhere more suitable to patronize.

We will all have noticed how the big catering companies have trained their staff to ask 'Is everything all right with your meal?'. The problem with this is making the question sound sincere: individual innkeepers can get a real competitive advantage from doing it better. Many customers find it difficult to complain and just say a meek 'Lovely, thank you' and never visit you again. Although it is not necessarily good policy to tease out complaints, it is often possible to see that things are not as good as they should be and suggest remedial action to the customer.

Flexibility is another way of avoiding complaints. How often have you been into an inn on the stroke of 2 pm only to be told that the kitchen is closed and they cannot even make you a sandwich in spite of the pub not closing for another thirty minutes. Try to put yourself in the position of the customer and try to help him, however inconvenient it might be.

Drinking-up time

Drinking-up time in pubs is not only a period when tempers get frayed but also a time when the goodwill earned throughout the evening is lost by clumsy snatching away of glasses or over zealousness in getting the premises clear. It is always worth remembering that you have been taking money from the customers all evening and that is the way they will feel too.

A home of your own

If you are not the owner of the pub or inn you are still likely to be living 'over the shop'. It is important on two counts, in our view, that you should start to purchase a private house of your own:

- Running a pub is a stressful and sometimes unpredictable business; things can go wrong for you or your family. You may wish to quit the tenancy, assign your lease or give up your job as a pub manager. You need a home to go to from which you can plan your new life, a safe haven after a possibly traumatic experience.
- Investing in a house, for most of the last fifty years, has been the best investment a family could make, in spite of the short hiccup in the late 1980s; the £20,000 home in 1970 might well be worth £200,000 today. You could be running a serious risk if you stay out of the housing market for too long.

Taking care of yourself and your family

It is often difficult, particularly when your business is not very buoyant, to make provision for the future. Take professional advice, make use of the tax benefits and do not leave it too late.

Life and critical illness insurance are not too expensive if you start them early enough. They do give you some protection in a business that is full of uncertainties.

Private health insurance is, if finances allow, worth the monthly investment. Unlike many of those in full-time employment your business dictates when you can and cannot take time off for an operation. You cannot just rely on staying healthy.

Summary

- We have tried in this chapter to give some practical advice on how to tackle the downsides of the trade.
- We hope you will not get a drug problem but, if you do, act at once.
- You may never get a violent incident but it can happen in any pub or inn at any time so be prepared.
- Customers are in short supply. Make sure they keep their driving licence and get home safely.
- Remember that you must always keep a clear head. It is not just customers who react out of character when they have drunk too much.
- Anticipate, do not wait for complaints or problems to happen. Get in first.
- Finally, plan for your future.

11 Keeping the law

The innkeeper is faced with a mass of legislation: that which is related specifically to licensed premises in addition to the many and various laws governing small businesses.

This chapter only aims to highlight certain areas of legislation which can cause difficulties for the innkeeper and to emphasize the dangers to the success or very existence of the business if the law is not observed.

Licensing law

To avoid committing serious offences against the Licensing Acts, the licensee **must not**:

- sell alcoholic liquor without a licence or on premises other than those authorized by the licence;
- sell alcoholic liquor of a kind not permitted by his/her licence;
- sell alcohol outside permitted hours;
- sell alcohol to a drunken person;
- knowingly sell alcohol to a person under eighteen or allow him or her to consume alcohol in the bar (but see the section **Children** below);
- allow drunkenness or disorderly conduct;
- allow prostitution or allow the licensed premises to be used as a brothel;

- allow passing of betting slips;
- allow unlawful gaming on the premises (traditional games of cribbage and dominoes may be played for small stakes but a serious offence would occur if, say, pontoon or other games of chance were being played for money in a bar);
- restrict the right of entry to the licensed premises in the course of their duty by a police officer or Customs and Excise official.

The licensee is also responsible for ensuring that his employees do not transgress the law.

There are numerous other offences under the Acts from 'allowing a police constable on duty to remain on licensed premises other than for carrying out his duties' to 'selling alcoholic drinks on credit other than to a resident or with a meal'.

The prudent innkeeper will have acquired and studied a summary of the licensing laws (for example *An ABC of Licensing Law* published by the *Licensee*) before applying for his/her first Justices' Licence – indeed, he or she may well be asked questions on aspects of the law by the magistrates when initially coming before them.

The licensing laws in Scotland differ from those in England and Wales in a number of important respects.

Children

There is probably more misunderstanding and argument about the status of children in pubs than there is about any other matter relating to licensing law.

In England and Wales, this vexed question revolves around what is and what is not a 'bar'. The definition of a bar in this context is 'any place exclusively or mainly used for the sale and consumption of intoxicating liquor'. Therefore, a room with a bar servery and tables and chairs mainly used by customers drinking is a 'bar' within the meaning of the Act. So is a separate room with no bar servery but where the main activity is drinking, the alcohol having been bought at a servery elsewhere on the premises or brought to the room by waiters or waitresses.

A room set up and used primarily for eating is not a 'bar' even though alcohol may be consumed as an ancillary to the meal.

The grey area is a room containing a bar servery where part of the room is used mainly by drinkers but part of the room mainly by diners. In these circumstances, the guidelines generally accepted by the Licensing Justices and the police are that the dining area should be sufficiently divorced from the bar servery and the drinkers as to form a defined entity even though there may be no solid dividing wall.

But be warned – the interpretation and definition of a 'bar' may vary widely from one licensing district or one police area to another so what may be acceptable in one is not acceptable in the other.

The reason for this concern about the definition of a 'bar' lies in the restrictions in the Licensing Acts on the admission of persons under eighteen into licensed premises.

The law in England and Wales may be summarized as follows:

Children under five

are not allowed to consume alcohol anywhere (except for medical reasons)

Children under fourteen

are not allowed in a bar
are not allowed to buy alcohol
are allowed in a room not designated as a bar
are allowed (if aged five or over) to drink alcohol with a meal in a room not designated as a bar

Children aged fourteen and fifteen

are allowed in a bar
are not allowed to drink alcohol in a bar
are not allowed to buy alcohol
are allowed to drink alcohol with a meal in a room not designated as a bar

Children aged sixteen and seventeen

are allowed in a bar

are not allowed to buy or to drink alcohol in a bar
are allowed to drink alcohol with a meal in a room not designated as a bar
are allowed to buy beer, porter, cider and perry for consumption with a meal on the premises in an area set aside mainly for the provision of food (i.e. not a bar).

Two further items to note: the licence-holder's children under fourteen are allowed in the bar; customers' children under fourteen are allowed to pass through a bar if this is the only practical access, e.g. to toilets.

A licensee has a degree of discretion and may find it prudent that even the lawful drinking, as described, by those under eighteen is discouraged. It is too easy for the finer points of the law to be misunderstood and the fifteen-year-old to boast to schoolfriends that he/she was drinking in your pub.

The commercial considerations

The whole question of children in pubs is an emotive one with parents often angry that the law does not allow them to take their younger children into a bar. Others argue that the bar is the last adult bastion and the law is protecting the traditional drinking environment.

You, as the licensee must observe the law but you may choose to add your own restrictions to suit the style of your business. For instance, you may believe that allowing those aged fourteen and up to eighteen into your bar would change its character and be detrimental to your trade – and therefore exclude them.

Others may take the view that adults with children represent good potential trade and do everything possible to encourage them, within legal limits.

It has to be said that there is a sizeable body of opinion which believes the present law in England and Wales is nonsensical and should be changed. This attitude is evident in the way that the police in many parts of the country apparently turn a blind eye to children being on licensed premises illegally. The Justices also seem to be more liberal in their interpretation of which areas of the pub or inn may be deemed not a bar within the meaning of the Act.

Children's Certificates

To meet the criticisms of the law relating to children in bars, Children's Certificates were introduced into Scotland and later, in January 1995, into England and Wales. They allow children under 14 in a bar if accompanied by an adult. Meals and 'beverages other than intoxicating liquor' must be available (but not necessarily consumed). The normal terminal hour is 9 pm.

Certificates are granted by the Licensing Justices who may impose such conditions as they think fit to ensure 'an environment in which it is suitable for persons under 14 to be present'. These conditions have sometimes caused great difficulty, when what many consider overburdensome and unnecessary demands have been made. The take up of Children's Certificates has therefore been slower than anticipated. One recent estimate is that only 5 per cent of English pubs have Children's Certificates.

Nevertheless, Children's Certificates can offer the opportunity for innkeepers wishing to develop family trade to make full use of the new law to build the business on an enlarged customer base.

Cigarettes

It is illegal to sell cigarettes to children under sixteen.

Permitted hours

It is clearly foolish for the innkeeper to put his/her precious Justices' Licence at risk by breaking the law but some do so, particularly in serving after hours. With the introduction of 'all day' opening (11 am to 11 pm Monday to Saturday and 12 noon to 10.30 pm on Sunday), the illegal afternoon late drinking session has disappeared but the temptation is still there for 'afters' at night.

We would argue that, quite apart from the legal aspect, this is ultimately an unproductive way to conduct the business. The house with a reputation for after-hours drinking will tend to find its customers arriving later and later so that the trade, instead of being additional, becomes merely a substitute. Meanwhile, the innkeeper is working longer hours, making an arduous day even more demanding and the following day's work more tiring.

'All day' opening has been a mixed blessing. It was a welcome relaxation of the licensing laws but relatively few pubs and inns have taken up the full 11 am to 11 pm opportunity – the reason being that, in many parts of the country, there is not the demand for alcohol through the afternoon.

However, when an innkeeper is setting out his or her stall and aiming for a target market, he or she now has the additional flexibility of using as many of the permitted hours as are profitable – and, most important, rejecting those afternoon hours when staff and other overheads outweigh any possible benefits.

Variations to permitted hours

Supper-hour certificate

A licensee with a restaurant or dining area may apply to the Licensing Justices for a certificate to serve alcohol **with meals** for an hour beyond normal closing time in the evening. Certain conditions have to be met but a supper-hour certificate can be a valuable asset to a pub restaurant in its bid to grow its business.

Extended hours order

For premises holding a supper-hour certificate, where not only meals but music or other entertainment is normally provided, an extended hours order may be granted which allows the permitted hours to extend up to 1 am for the provision of liquor to customers enjoying meals and entertainment.

Special hours certificate

If premises are suitable, the licensee has a full licence and an Entertainment Licence (see below) and provides music and dancing as well as meals, a special hours certificate may be applied for. This certificate may extend permitted hours to 2 am (3 am in London) subject to any restrictions set by the Justices.

As we go to press this traditional interpretation of special hours is being challenged through the courts. The alternative legal view is that if a pub obtains 'special hours' after 11 pm it must close during the day. We anticipate that the House of Lords will rule that this latter view is a nonsense.

Occasional licence

If you wish to run a bar at a function, such as a dance at the village hall, you must apply to the Licensing Magistrates for an occasional licence. The licensing laws, in most respects, govern the bar at the function as they do for a bar in a pub. Always remember that you, as licensee, will be held responsible for any problems that arise at an outside function, so ensure that you supervise it.

Entertainment licences

These are granted by Local Authorities in England and Wales to those premises wishing to provide live music by more than two performers or to provide facilities for dancing.

Before applying for such a licence, the licensee should judge carefully the benefits because the costs can often be considerable. The premises are inspected for their suitability and extremely strict provisions are made for their safety, particularly with regard to fire. It is more than likely that additional fire exits, fire-resistant doors and fire-fighting equipment and procedures will be demanded. In addition, a restriction on numbers allowed on the premises will be enforced and this may well be a lower number than is on the premises already on a busy night.

Finally, there is no fixed fee for an Entertainment Licence; some Local Authorities have set their fees at a high level.

Unless you can see a radical increase in your trade, you should seriously consider restricting your entertainment to two live performers in any one session – it might save you a lot of money in the long run!

Liquor – volumes

Many drinks may only be sold in the permitted measures.

- Draught beer and cider – one-third pint, half-pint or multiples of half-pint, served by metered dispense (in which case the meter must be government stamped) or served free flow in glasses which are government stamped. It is legal at present (although still a matter of controversy in some quarters) for draught beers and ciders to be served with a 'head' in a brim-measure glass, providing that the head does not exceed 5 per cent of the total volume. It is an offence to serve under-measure but the over-measure and long pull, while not illegal, could severely damage the bank balance. The exception to the above is when a mixed drink such as shandy is served. You may use a pint or a half-pint glass but the drink should be described on the price list as simply large or small.
- Spirits – gin, whisky, rum and vodka may only be sold in specified quantities either through a sealed and stamped optic or a stamped thimble measure (except for use in cocktails with three or more liquid ingredients). The historic Imperial measures have been replaced by metric measures (25 ml or multiples thereof). The licensee must display notices stating the measures in use on the premises.
- Wine – still table wines may only be sold by the glass in measures of 125 ml or 175 ml or multiples thereof. A notice must be displayed stating which measure or measures are being used.

Liquor – quality

The licensee is governed by the same laws concerning quality as any other retailer. The goods sold must be what they purport to be. Watered beer or diluted spirits are clearly illegal, and a successful prosecution against a publican may result in loss of licence and reputation. Watering of beer or spirits is particularly mean as those being cheated are the customers who are supporting the pub or inn: an exact opposite to customer care!

It is also illegal to 'pass off' products. If the customer asks for Gordons gin or Britvic orange, you must not give him alternative brands without his or her knowledge and acceptance. Similarly, if the menu says 'scampi', then scampi it must be and not some other fish product hiding beneath the crisp coating. Frozen Canadian salmon sold as 'fresh Scottish salmon' is 'passing off' and is a prosecutable offence.

Price marking

By law, you must display individual prices or a price list for your products in a prominent position in your bar or each bar. These must be easy for the average customer to read and it is illegal to charge different prices from those displayed. If you have fewer than thirty items for a menu or bar price list you have to display the price of them all; more than thirty items and you need only price a minimum of thirty representative items.

All food and drink prices must include VAT (assuming the premises are VAT registered). You may use chalk boards to cover additional items or to highlight products you wish to especially push. Wines by the bottle for sale in the bar or restaurant must also be priced on an appropriate list. Similarly, food prices, whether bar snacks or a full restaurant menu, must also be readily available to the public before ordering. Again, a chalk board has become an effective and popular way of displaying food prices.

Whether a price list or menu is hand-written or printed, good marketing demands that it should be appropriate for its setting, well-organized, neat and easy to read. An over-elaborately produced menu can create as unfavourable an impression as a scruffy one. It also goes without saying that it must be up-to-date and not full of alterations and crossings-out.

Employment legislation

The innkeeper who employs staff needs to be aware of the weight of legislation on this issue and must keep up-to-date because some of the rules change from year to year.

Once an employee earns over the currently specified amount and is deemed to be in regular employment, the employer must deduct Income Tax and National Insurance Contributions (NIC) and, with the employer's NIC, remit the sums to the Tax Office, usually monthly.

The employer must, when taking on an employee:

- tell the local Tax Office;
- record earnings and deductions;
- tell the Tax Office the total of these earnings and deductions each year;
- keep these records for three years;
- record employee's name and address.

The Tax Office will explain how to calculate PAYE, and the Department of Social Security (DSS) how to work out NIC.

The employee who works over eight hours a week is entitled to receive, within thirteen weeks of starting, a written statement of his or her terms of employment covering:

- name of employer;
- job title and description;
- hours of work;
- pay details;
- holiday entitlement;
- sickness or injury procedures;
- grievance procedures;
- length of notice;

- pension scheme (where applicable);
- disciplinary rules.

This last is useful where the employer has, for instance, dress rules which he wishes to record and formalize.

The Contract of Employment is the reference point in any dispute and needs to be thought through carefully.

In particular, dismissal of staff must be approached with great caution. In the unhappy event that a member of staff has to be dismissed, the employer must follow full and proper procedures to the letter. Even what you consider to be a blatant act justifying dismissal, such as theft of stock, can turn against you if you act outside the law protecting the employee. Statutory compensation or awards for unfair dismissal can be costly.

If in doubt about any of these employment matters seek professional advice from the relevant government department or, as a last resort, a solicitor.

Disability Discrimination Act

Employers (except those employing fewer than twenty people, full or part-time) and people that provide goods and services to the public must take reasonable measures to ensure that disabled people are not discriminated against, although employers are still able to recruit or promote the best person for the job.

The key word here is 'reasonable'. Helpful leaflets about this relatively new legislation can be obtained from the Department for Education and Employment.

Other employee-protection legislation

- You must not discriminate on grounds of sex, colour or race.
- You must offer equal pay to men and women for equivalent work and observe any legislation relating to the minimum hourly rate or wage.

- Expectant mothers are entitled to maternity leave in certain employment situations (check with the DSS).
- Statutory Sick Pay may be due to your staff (check with the DSS).
- Children under eighteen (even the licensee's children) may not be employed in a bar unless they are sixteen- or seventeen-year olds on an Approved Apprenticeship Scheme. Your local Training and Enterprise Council (TEC) should be able to give further details or refer you to a training provider (e.g. Hotel and Catering Training Company).
- The employer must have valid employer's liability insurance and display the certificate of insurance on the premises.

There is a helpful series of leaflets available from the Department for Education and Employment.

Health and safety

If five or more employees work at the premises, the inn must have a health and safety document which sets out the policy for establishing safe and legal working conditions. The innkeeper has the responsibility for ensuring the policy is carried out.

Regardless of the size of the premises or number of employees, the innkeeper must ensure that the working conditions for his or her employees are safe as reasonably possible and that the customers are not exposed to avoidable risk. So loose stair treads, broken lino, exposed cutting edges and insecure stepladders are all examples of bad practice which could lead to accidents, possible legal action and heavy costs.

It is the employer's responsibility to provide proper training and supervision for staff in health and safety at work.

The local Health and Safety Executive gives advice and literature on safe and legal working conditions. The Environmental Health Department of the local authority is responsible for inspecting premises and also gives helpful advice.

Fire precautions

A vital part of safety procedures is precautions against fire. The innkeeper must ensure there are appropriate and adequate means of escape for staff and customers, that exit routes are not blocked or inaccessible and that there is suitable fire-fighting equipment kept in good order.

A **Fire Certificate** is required for premises:

- where there are twenty or more employees (at any one time) or ten or more other than on the ground floor;
- where six or more people (guests and/or staff) have sleeping accommodation;
- where there is sleeping accommodation above first-floor or below ground-floor level;
- where an Entertainment Licence is required (see the section earlier in this chapter).

The innkeeper should be aware that it is a serious offence to employ staff in premises requiring a Fire Certificate if one has not been granted. No chances can be taken with fire hazards – if in doubt, you must contact your local Fire Authority.

If you are operating in premises you do not own where the landlord has legal responsibility for aspects of the building's maintenance, you need to inform the landlord immediately (and confirm in writing) of any defect or hazard which could be his or her responsibility to rectify under any of the various Acts concerned with health and safety.

Food hygiene

Food premises (remember drink is food) are required to be registered with the Local Authority.

Appropriate authorized training in hygiene must be undertaken by food handlers (take advice from your local Environmental Health Department).

The innkeeper must take all reasonable steps to ensure that the food served is safe: therefore it must be stored at the correct temperature, kept free from contamination and handled hygienically from purchase to the customer's plate (or glass).

The EHO's advice is invaluable and could be critical to the success or failure of your business.

As we stressed in Chapter 9, food safety now has an extremely high profile throughout the country. You are in the spotlight; take no chances, get everything right, be careful, be thorough, and be safe.

Control of Substances Hazardous to Health (COSHH)

Legislation has been in existence since 1990 which makes it an offence for an employee to be exposed to any substance hazardous to health unless the employer has completed an assessment of risk and made sure adequate controls are observed.

This complicated piece of legislation means that an innkeeper must define products on the premises that may be hazardous, e.g. oven cleaner, toilet cleaner, dishwasher detergent, CO_2. For the benefit of the employees, he or she must list the products by name, explain the possible hazard(s) and show the precautions which must be taken. He/she may have to provide protective clothing in some instances and, for this purpose as well as for other legislation, appropriate first-aid.

Reporting

There are a number of circumstances affecting employees in which an employer has responsibility for reporting to the Local Authority including:

- fatal or specified serious accidents at work;
- dangerous occurrences at work;

- accidents at work causing more than three consecutive days' incapacity for work;
- reportable specified illnesses in food handlers likely to cause food poisoning (in which case the employee must stop work and the employer report the illness to the Local Medical Officer of Health).

Building controls

Over the years, large sums of money have been wasted by licensees because they rushed ahead with alterations to the pub without understanding the legal requirements.

Tenants and lessees must read the agreements with their landlords and only make alterations or improvements to the building with the landlord's permission.

All licensees need to observe:

- **Building Regulations** which are designed, among other things, to guarantee the safety of the building.
- **Planning laws** which preserve the appearance and fitness of the building within its environment.
- **Listed building legislation** which protects buildings having notable architectural or historic features.

It is most unwise for any innkeeper to start knocking out walls, altering windows or making similar structural changes without getting qualified advice. It may be more expensive to start with but can save a fortune in the longer run.

Last but not least, the Licensing Justices need to approve in advance any alterations you are planning which affect the layout or service in the non-domestic areas of the pub. They are concerned particularly with facilities for the public and staff including toilets; the degree of supervision available to the licensees; safety and, of course, observation of the law.

In many cases, especially in old buildings, the Justices have accepted a situation because of long-standing physical limitations of the premises. However, if plans are submitted for alterations, you may well find that the Justices ask for unexpected extra facilities. For instance, a modest plan to take a six square metre storeroom into the bar and use it for extra dining space may lead to a request for additional ladies' lavatories.

If an innkeeper fails to apply for permission or asks for permission retrospectively, the Licensing Justices have to revoke the licence. They may subsequently renew it but, if they are not satisfied that it was a genuine mistake, the pub licence could be temporarily or permanently lost.

Plans

Plans submitted to the Licensing Justices normally have to have copies sent to the police, the Local Authority and the Fire Authority, any of which may have grounds for objection.

Failure to get all the appropriate approvals before going ahead with alterations or additions can lead to your having to reinstate the premises and, in extreme circumstances, to the loss of your licence.

We have said it before, but it is worth repeating: take qualified advice before you start on alterations and continue to observe the law at every stage until completion. Getting it wrong can be very expensive indeed!

Transfer of undertaking regulations

These Regulations can be a major problem for a new owner taking over an inn if he or she is not aware of their implications.

You, as the new owner, take over the existing staff on their present terms and conditions. Any years of service with the previous owner or owners count as continuous service with you. It is important, therefore, that you get full employment details from the previous owner as length of service is a key factor in determining employees' rights, for instance, to redundancy pay or maternity pay and the right to return to work.

Employees dismissed before or after the transfer will be considered as unfairly dismissed unless legal grounds as specified in the Regulations can be proved to apply – failure to have these grounds can lead to an expensive claim against you.

Changes in terms and conditions need to be negotiated and agreed, not imposed.

Understand the Regulations and act within the law – if in doubt, take qualified advice.

Landlord and Tenant Act

Tenancies of public houses (other than those for a term less than six months) are now covered by the Act.

This offers greater security of tenure and protection by the courts for a tenant who wishes to remain on the premises. There are only certain grounds on which a landlord can base a claim to terminate the tenancy. If they do so, compensation is due to the tenant.

Although this change in the law has long been sought by tenants' licensed trade bodies, it has also contributed to the major brewers' switching from rolling one-year agreements to ten- or twenty-year leases – not seen by everyone as the great leap forward it was purported to be at the time.

Innkeepers

Throughout this book, we use the word 'innkeeper' in its popular sense as the licensee of a public house or inn with the implication that food, as well as drink, will be served in the establishment.

But there is a narrow legal definition under the *Hotel Proprietors Act* 1956 as one who offers food, drink and sleeping accommodation to travellers, day or night. Provided that they can pay, are in a fit state and the house is not full, the innkeeper is obliged to take them. He must take all reasonable care of his guests' possessions and has a lien on them to cover his fair charges (but guests' vehicles and their contents are not included). The inn must be as safe as the innkeeper can reasonably make it for the guests use.

The innkeeper can limit their liability for loss or damage to guests' possessions by prominently displaying the appropriate schedule from the Act. Also, it is prudent for the innkeeper to display a disclaimer notice in their car park (although it does not necessarily absolve them in law) such as:

> No liability can be accepted
> for loss or damage to
> cars or their contents

Innkeepers must keep a register of the name and address and date of arrival of British guests staying at the inn and, in the form prescribed by the Secretary of State, keep a register of aliens aged sixteen or over, retaining such a register for at least twelve months.

Summary

This chapter may leave you feeling overwhelmed by the sheer volume of legislation under which your business has to labour. You may wish to complain to your Trade Association or MP about laws you think unfairly oppressive on the small businessman or businesswoman but, while laws are on the statute book, you cannot afford to ignore them.

- Make it a priority to understand the basic legislation and the way it affects you.
- Work within the law, do not try to circumvent it.
- Consult all the sources of free advice when you need them – Inland Revenue, Department for Education and Employment, Department for Social Security and Environmental Health Departments etc.
- Take skilled advice – from accountants, solicitors, architects and other professionals – whenever necessary: good advice is never expensive in the long run.
- Stay in control of your business at all times.

12 A way of life

Throughout this book, we have taken pains to stress the need for professionalism. Running a pub or inn is not something to be undertaken without thorough understanding of everything that is involved – including the key questions of location, accurate targeting of customers, satisfying those customers' needs through creating the right ambience, offering the appropriate products and training staff to the highest standards of customer care.

The best pubs and inns are those where the licensee is in personal charge and impresses his or her character, skill and enthusiasm on all aspects of the business, both out front and behind the scenes.

That elusive element, 'atmosphere', which always scores highly when customers are polled on what they look for in a favourite inn, is created by the innkeeper. A successful pub can change owners and see a big drop in trade although nothing physically has altered – but the customers sense a loss of atmosphere. The reverse can equally well happen: new owners can transform an ailing business through understanding their market and creating the atmosphere which appeals to customers.

'Atmosphere' is not a thing of chance – it comes about because all the complex features that go into the make-up of the British pub are brought together in one building by the efforts of a team of people who clearly understand the fundamental purpose of the business. Leading that team is the successful innkeeper.

Creating success is one thing; keeping it going is another. Many inns have a wonderful flowering where new owners get everything right and the public flock to enjoy the experience of eating and drinking there. In a disappointing number of cases, the early success is not sustained. Why?

We believe that, for the owners, either boredom sets in after the initial creative excitement or complacency, because the business grew so quickly and apparently easily.

The difficult step to take is from the early stage of novelty, innovation and business-building to the mature stage of an established, solidly based, continuously successful, thriving enterprise.

This desirable state of affairs is brought about by the unglamorous but essential ability of the innkeeper to produce a consistent performance session after session, day after day, month in, month out – what we have referred to before as 'doing the milking'. This means that the innkeeper must always be on top of the job, always maintain standards, always be aware of the staff's performance and the customers' needs so that the 'product' – food, drink and service plus atmosphere – is of consistently high quality.

The seven-day week of the licensed trade and the long hours demand professionalism of a high order, as well as organizational ability to make full use of the twenty-four hours in each day.

We give below an example of a typical weekday in the life of a husband and wife team (with no children but a large dog) running a traditional food-led inn with the support of a small staff. The pub closes in the afternoon from 3 pm to 6 pm.

A typical day – John Jones, The White Hart

7 am:	Get up
7.30 am:	Walk dog
8 am:	Breakfast – read post Read papers including trade papers
8.45 am:	Bookwork including enter yesterday's takings, payments – deal with day's post
9.15 am:	Telephone calls with suppliers etc.
9.30 am:	Drive to bank (five miles away), pay in takings
10.10 am:	Return to inn – check cellar, ensure draught beers are ready to serve, check bar stock, put up spirits, wine and cigarettes [N.B. cleaner cleans kitchen, bars, loos, cellar, takes out empties, stocks up bottled beers, soft drinks]
10.35 am:	Shower, change
10.55 am:	Bring till drawers and floats from safe
11 am:	Open inn, run bar on own until 11.45 am when barman takes over
11.45 am:	Light lunch
12.15 pm to 3.15 pm:	Run bar with staff. Take opportunities to circulate in bar and dining area
3.15 pm to 3.45 pm:	Help clean, tidy bar. Stock up bar for evening. Check cellar. Check cash against till readings, put cash and till drawers in safe. Float tills for evening. Check loos, car park, exterior, security
3.45 pm to 5.15 pm:	Upstairs for rest
5.15 pm:	Walk dog
5.45 pm:	Set up cellar for evening session
5.55 pm:	Till drawers and floats from safe

6 pm:	Open inn, run bar on own until 7 pm when barman takes over
7 pm to 7.30 pm:	Evening meal
7.30 pm:	Break
7.45 pm to 11.20 pm:	Run bar with staff. Circulate in bar and dining area
11.20 pm to 11.40 pm:	Check cash against till readings. Cash and till drawers to safe. Check cellar. Check loos, car park, exterior, security
11.40 pm:	Upstairs for rest, pot of tea, sandwich
12.15 am:	Bed

A typical day – Jane Jones, The White Hart

7 am:	Get up
7.30 am:	Prepare breakfast, read papers, trade papers, post
7.55 am:	Let in cleaner, brief on specific requirements
8 am:	Breakfast
8.30 am:	Let in two kitchen staff, brief on morning's work (N.B. one member of kitchen staff is general assistant, the other more skilled, being trained up as a cook)
8.45 am to 9.30 am:	Visit fresh food suppliers
9.30 am:	Work on menu planning, telephone calls with suppliers etc.
10 am to 11.30 am:	Work in kitchen with staff, check in food deliveries
11.30 am to 12 noon:	Shower, change
12 noon to 2.30 pm:	Supervise and work in kitchen, handle waitresses, food bills, payments
2.30 pm to 3 pm:	With staff, prepare food for evening session. Stock up fridges, freezers etc.

3 pm to 3.30 pm:	Lunch
3.30 pm:	Upstairs for rest
5 pm:	Domestic chores [N.B. Cleaning lady for private quarters two mornings a week]
6 pm:	Shower, change
6.45 pm to 10 pm:	Supervise and work in kitchen, handle waitresses, food bills, payments
10 pm:	With staff, clear up kitchen ready for morning
10.30 pm:	Out front with customers
11.15 pm:	Upstairs for rest, pot of tea, sandwich
12.15 am:	Bed

This would be a daunting day for most people outside the trade. The point to stress is that this is not an exceptional day, this is the norm. Other days, weekends or Bank Holidays might well be tougher.

Our view is that to be a publican or innkeeper, is one of the most demanding jobs anyone can take on. To be a successful publican or innkeeper is even more difficult and to be consistently successful demands a personality, skill and enthusiasm given to relatively few. It is no wonder that, at any one time, of Britain's more than 58,000 pubs and inns, there is always a considerable percentage which falls far short of the highest standards and traditions. The room for improvement is there for all to see.

If standards are not kept high and customers and potential customers do not perceive the British pub as any longer offering good value, then the institution will wither away.

We are optimistic enough to believe that the trade will be sufficiently resilient to survive and, indeed, flourish but inevitably with a smaller number of outlets. The pubs and inns that succeed should be very good indeed for they will be contenders in a leisure market of intense competitiveness.

Our belief is supported by the uniqueness of the British pub as an institution and the expectation that there will always be those individuals who rise to the challenge of innkeeping and create the perfect pub.

The innkeeper who is successful, who has moulded the business into exactly the shape planned and then experiences the rewards, not just financial, of customers choosing to come to his or her inn to eat and drink, to enjoy the atmosphere he or she has created, can feel an intense pleasure in achievement and, in a tiny way, can justifiably believe that his or her efforts have added to the sum of human happiness.

It is these men and women, successful publicans or innkeepers, who know that they are enjoying the best job in the world.

Index

SUCCESSFUL PUBS AND INNS